An Analysis of

J. A. Hobson's

Imperialism
A Study

Riley Quinn

ROUTLEDGE

www.macat.com
info@macat.com

Cover illustration: Etienne Gilfillan

Cataloguing in Publication Data
A catalogue record for this book is available from the British Library.
Library of Congress Cataloguing-in-Publication Data is available upon request.

ISBN 978-1-912303-29-8 (hardback)
ISBN 978-1-912128-65-5 (paperback)
ISBN 978-1-912282-17-3 (e-book)

Notice
The information in this book is designed to orientate readers of the work under analysis,
to elucidate and contextualise its key ideas and themes, and to aid in the development
of critical thinking skills. It is not meant to be used, nor should it be used, as a
substitute for original thinking or in place of original writing or research. References and
notes are provided for informational purposes and their presence does not constitute
endorsement of the information or opinions therein. This book is presented solely for
educational purposes. It is sold on the understanding that the publisher is not engaged
to provide any scholarly advice. The publisher has made every effort to ensure that
this book is accurate and up-to-date, but makes no warranties or representations with
regard to the completeness or reliability of the information it contains. The information
and the opinions provided herein are not guaranteed or warranted to produce particular
results and may not be suitable for students of every ability. The publisher shall not be
liable for any loss, damage or disruption arising from any errors or omissions, or from
the use of this book, including, but not limited to, special, incidental, consequential or
other damages caused, or alleged to have been caused, directly or indirectly, by the
information contained within.

CONTENTS

THE MACAT LIBRARY

The Macat Library is a series of unique academic explorations of seminal works in the humanities and social sciences – books and papers that have had a significant and widely recognised impact on their disciplines. It has been created to serve as much more than just a summary of what lies between the covers of a great book. It illuminates and explores the influences on, ideas of, and impact of that book. Our goal is to offer a learning resource that encourages critical thinking and fosters a better, deeper understanding of important ideas.

Each publication is divided into three Sections: Influences, Ideas, and Impact. Each Section has four Modules. These explore every important facet of the work, and the responses to it.

This Section-Module structure makes a Macat Library book easy to use, but it has another important feature. Because each Macat book is written to the same format, it is possible (and encouraged!) to cross-reference multiple Macat books along the same lines of inquiry or research. This allows the reader to open up interesting interdisciplinary pathways.

To further aid your reading, lists of glossary terms and people mentioned are included at the end of this book (these are indicated by an asterisk [*] throughout) – as well as a list of works cited.

Macat has worked with the University of Cambridge to identify the elements of critical thinking and understand the ways in which six different skills combine to enable effective thinking.
Three allow us to fully understand a problem; three more give us the tools to solve it. Together, these six skills make up the **PACIER** model of critical thinking. They are:

ANALYSIS – understanding how an argument is built
EVALUATION – exploring the strengths and weaknesses of an argument
INTERPRETATION – understanding issues of meaning

CREATIVE THINKING – coming up with new ideas and fresh connections
PROBLEM-SOLVING – producing strong solutions
REASONING – creating strong arguments

To find out more, visit **WWW.MACAT.COM.**

CRITICAL THINKING AND *IMPERIALISM*

Primary critical thinking skill: ANALYSIS
Secondary critical thinking skill: EVALUATION

English economist John Hobson's 1902 *Imperialism: A Study* was an epoch-making study of the politics and economics of imperialism that shook imperialist beliefs to their core. A committed liberal, Hobson was deeply sceptical about the aims and claims of imperialistic thought at a time when Britain's empire held sway over a vast portion of the globe. In order to critique what he saw as a falsely reasoned and immoral political view, Hobson's book took a cuttingly analytical approach to the idea of imperialism. One of his key insights was to evaluate arguments surrounding the origins of imperialism – a process in which he found the widely accepted claims that imperialism was essentially a question of nationalism to be, in fact, quite weak. Instead, his close analysis of the implicit and hidden reasons behind nationalism demonstrated that, at root, it was a product of capitalism. In his analysis, it becomes clear that less than a political ideology, imperialism stems from the need to open up new markets, and remedy economic stagnation. Deeply provocative at the time, Hobson's book shows just how powerful analysis and evaluation can be at deconstructing the most widely accepted of ideas.

ABOUT THE AUTHOR OF THE ORIGINAL WORK

The political economist **John A. Hobson** was born in 1858 to a middle class family in Derbyshire, England. His father was a newspaper owner, and Hobson eventually became a journalist himself. As South Africa correspondent for the Manchester Guardian, he covered the Second Boer War at the very end of the nineteenth century. It was here that he began to develop his radical theories about how capitalism drove a nation's desire for empire building. Hobson died in 1940, two years after publishing his autobiography Confessions of an Economic Heretic.

ABOUT THE AUTHOR OF THE ANALYSIS

Riley Quinn holds master's degrees in politics and international relations from both LSE and the University of Oxford.

ABOUT MACAT

GREAT WORKS FOR CRITICAL THINKING

Macat is focused on making the ideas of the world's great thinkers accessible and comprehensible to everybody, everywhere, in ways that promote the development of enhanced critical thinking skills.

It works with leading academics from the world's top universities to produce new analyses that focus on the ideas and the impact of the most influential works ever written across a wide variety of academic disciplines. Each of the works that sit at the heart of its growing library is an enduring example of great thinking. But by setting them in context – and looking at the influences that shaped their authors, as well as the responses they provoked – Macat encourages readers to look at these classics and game-changers with fresh eyes. Readers learn to think, engage and challenge their ideas, rather than simply accepting them.

'Macat offers an amazing first-of-its-kind tool for interdisciplinary learning and research. Its focus on works that transformed their disciplines and its rigorous approach, drawing on the world's leading experts and educational institutions, opens up a world-class education to anyone.'

Andreas Schleicher
Director for Education and Skills, Organisation for Economic
Co-operation and Development

'Macat is taking on some of the major challenges in university education … They have drawn together a strong team of active academics who are producing teaching materials that are novel in the breadth of their approach.'

Prof Lord Broers,
former Vice-Chancellor of the University of Cambridge

'The Macat vision is exceptionally exciting. It focuses upon new modes of learning which analyse and explain seminal texts which have profoundly influenced world thinking and so social and economic development. It promotes the kind of critical thinking which is essential for any society and economy. This is the learning of the future.'

Rt Hon Charles Clarke, former UK Secretary of State for Education

'The Macat analyses provide immediate access to the critical conversation surrounding the books that have shaped their respective discipline, which will make them an invaluable resource to all of those, students and teachers, working in the field.'

Professor William Tronzo, University of California at San Diego

WAYS IN TO THE TEXT

KEY POINTS

- John Hobson (1858–1940) was an English economist and political thinker.
- Published in 1902, his book *Imperialism: A Study* argued that international aggression resulted from domestic economic conditions.
- Hobson was among the first to argue that a direct connection existed between inequality and aggressive foreign policy, and to further connect this to undue influence wielded by the wealthy and politically connected. This is as relevant now as it was to nineteenth-century England.

Who Was John Hobson?

John Hobson, the author of *Imperialism: A Study* (1902), was born in 1858 in the English county of Derbyshire and died in 1940. He studied Classics—that is, ancient Greek and Latin literature—at Oxford University, before beginning a career as a journalist. His family had been involved in the newspaper industry his entire life; indeed, his father owned one of Derbyshire's newspapers. He wrote for the *Manchester Guardian*, which in 1959 became the *Guardian*, a paper that remains globally important today. One of his most important jobs for the *Manchester Guardian* was to cover the Boer War,* a conflict between Britain and the descendants of Dutch settlers in what is today South Africa.

Hobson, a public intellectual, was a member of many famous "ethical" clubs in London and was associated with the socialist* Fabian Society,* which famously founded the London School of Economics (a prestigious seat of learning in London). While attending meetings of these societies, Hobson wrote many articles for liberal* weekly journals (that is, journals that shared his political beliefs about liberty and social justice). His experiences in southern Africa, and his work with the ethical societies, shaped his argument in *Imperialism*. More than just a liberal thinker, Hobson was an economist of some note as well. He and his friend Albert Mummery,* a businessman and mountain climber, wrote a book called *The Physiology of Industry* that was an important criticism of most economic theory at the time.

As he saw European nations turn from dominating the world to destroying one another in World War I,* his view of human nature became less economic and more personal; his experiences as a European public intellectual eventually led him to distrust human nature.

What Does *Imperialism* Say?
Hobson intended *Imperialism* to answer one main question: What is the rationale behind an imperial foreign policy—that is, a foreign policy aimed at empire building?

The consensus then was that conquering foreign lands would expand trade, thus enriching everyone—a belief summed up by the phrase "trade follows the flag." Hobson challenged this belief by showing that taking new land had no effect on trade. And given that the British Empire was expensive to maintain in terms of both money and manpower, he looked for other explanations for the imperial project.

Hobson argued that the empire did make economic sense—but only for a very small number of wealthy capitalists* (that is, roughly speaking, investors and business owners). He came to this conclusion through a purely economic argument.

Hobson's theory of "oversaving," which he developed alongside his friend Mummery, held that some people kept too much money for themselves. This money was not reinvested into the economy, and more and more was held up in savings accounts. They reasoned that the rich would not invest it in things such as factories because many people were too poor to buy the things the factories made. The rich, then, bought things abroad, such as mines and railroads, as better investments. But since the wider world was not as safe as Britain, Hobson argued that rich people used their political connections to promote imperial policy.

Hobson thought that if wealth were redistributed, poor people would hold enough money at home that the rich could invest their money profitably without needing to look abroad. He called this redistribution "social reform" and based it on the idea of "social liberalism"*—the belief that organs of the state should guarantee the liberty of the citizen. This point of view emphasizes the rights of the community to live a good life, where their needs are met; government policy benefitting only a very few people was not only undemocratic, but also profoundly harmful to ordinary Britons.

There was also an important second part to this argument: the moral problems of imperialism,* the policy of subjugating territories abroad for economic gain.

Even if imperialism had no economic grounds, people still tried to justify it as a moral project on the grounds that Europeans were obliged to "civilize the savage." Hobson argued that arguments such as these were simply a cover for the economic ambitions of the empire, pointing out the ways in which imperialists chose domination over the process of civilization. This marked a key difference between "colonizing" (where the rights enjoyed by the civilized are extended to new lands) and "imperializing" (where one group is exploited by another outside its borders).

Imperialism did not only pose a problem for the dominated: for Hobson, imperial policy hurt British culture, too. He thought imperialism made British society more military—and that good soldiers, required to learn a forceful attitude where problems were solved by violence rather than dialogue, were not necessarily good citizens. Politicians who learned their trade in the empire, Hobson argued, were more likely to oppress citizens at home than those who learned in the UK.

Why Does *Imperialism* Matter?

According to Hobson, "financiers"—that is, people who make their living from investments—wield a disproportionate amount of power in the imperial project. But he does not adequately explain who, precisely, he means by this. Moreover, it can be argued that the line Hobson draws between capitalism* and imperialism is questionably straight. For students, then, the book provides an excellent case study of attractive but overly simple reasoning that does not, perhaps, take account of the complexity of the real world.

Although Hobson's theory was largely rejected by his peers, Marxist* scholars turned to it, giving it some prominence. As people whose analysis of society was inspired by the theories of the economist and social theorist Karl Marx,* they agreed with Hobson that imperialism was bound to arise from capitalism (the economic system dominant today throughout the West and much of the developing world). They differed from Hobson, however, in their belief that the solution lay in revolution rather than reform.

Throughout the twentieth century, Hobson continued to influence political thinkers, inspired by his criticism of empire, but critics of imperial policy in the modern era bear little direct similarity to Hobson. Where he examined the role of a narrowly defined group of investors in perpetrating imperialism, political philosophers and thinkers such as the American literary theorist and philosopher Michael Hardt* and the Marxist philosopher Antonio Negri* consider imperialism as a kind of "state of mind." For them, imperialism is an idea that defines all social relations around the world—a great broadening of the term's use and implications.

Moreover, modern readers would look at Hobson's moral qualifications regarding imperialism with some skepticism; he believes, for example, that imperialism is moral when it involves "spreading civilization." Implying that one society is superior to another, this is no longer a persuasive argument.

While some of Hobson's ideas have fallen out of favor, the general direction of his theory remains much more important. *Imperialism*, read more generally, examines the connection between economic and political concerns. The politically and financially well connected can shape the world to their ends—and even though Hobson's argument does not prove this perfectly, the argument did help inspire a generation of scholars. Some of the most important twentieth-century theorists who followed in Hobson's footsteps were Marxists, who looked at the ways imperialism continues under different names. Hobson's arguments can give students a new perspective on the ways in which powerful countries acquired spheres of influence in the Cold War* (the period of tension between the Soviet Union and its allies and the United States and its allies in the years between 1947 and 1991).

Moreover, *Imperialism* can help readers learn to cast doubt on the justifications given to support foreign aggression; even if reading Hobson does not give us a coherent theory of *why* imperial policy occurs, it can give us a sense of *how* political statements spin reality into something that is not always as it seems.

SECTION 1
INFLUENCES

MODULE 1
THE AUTHOR AND THE
HISTORICAL CONTEXT

KEY POINTS

- *Imperialism* retains its importance for study because it draws out moral and economic arguments for the economic rationale of international aggression.

- Hobson was a member of many left-wing societies, and worked as a journalist for left-wing newspapers covering the Boer War* (a British attempt to seize control of much of modern South Africa from the Boers—the descendants of Dutch settlers).

- European states engaged in a "scramble" for foreign lands in the nineteenth century.

Why Read This Text?

In his 1902 book *Imperialism: A Study*, the British economist and radical* reformer John Hobson argued that imperialism*—the policy of "empire building" in foreign territories—was a negative force both at home in Britain and in Britain's possessions abroad. Here, "radical" refers to a tradition in left-wing British politics committed to social justice through social reform.

Hobson's book stood out from other anti-imperialist writings because his argument was both ethical and economic. He set out not only to condemn imperial policy as immoral, but also to show that it was bad for the welfare of most citizens of the imperial state.

Contrary to the then popular assertion that "trade follows the flag" (meaning that extending Britain's empire meant extending Britain's trade base as well, supposedly improving life for everybody),[1] Hobson

> **❝** What is attractive is Hobson's ability to separate and disassemble the interests of the commercial and imperial aims. He makes the valid point that other European countries, without the benefit of empires, manage to be successful trading and industrial powers in their own right. **❞**
>
> Jeremy Corbyn, "Introduction," *Imperialism: A Study*

argued that imperialism served to protect major capital investments abroad for the benefit of a "parasitic" class of ultra-wealthy financiers* at the taxpayer's expense.[2] Here, "capital investments" refers, simply, to money used to generate profit through investment—which is what financiers do for a living.

Hobson, who was to describe himself as an "economic heretic," should be remembered for his originality. *Imperialism* is no exception. "What was controversial at the time," wrote the British politician Jeremy Corbyn* in the introduction to the 2011 edition of *Imperialism*, "is his analysis of the pressures that were hard at work in pushing for a vast national effort in grabbing new outposts of empire."[3]

Author's Life

Hobson was born in 1858 to a middle-class family in the county of Derbyshire, England; his father was a prosperous newspaper owner. He started at Oxford University in 1876, where he read Classics (ancient Latin and Greek literature), although he developed an interest in philosophy and political economy* (a branch of the study of economics focused on the ways in which politics affects real economic outcomes) outside his studies.

On moving back to London, Hobson became a journalist and a lecturer; eventually he was sent to what is today South Africa to cover the Boer War,* a conflict fought in the years 1899–1902 between the

British Empire and the descendants of Dutch settlers known as the Boers. As a journalist and something of a public intellectual, Hobson was a prolific writer of short essays and articles. *Imperialism* is, in fact, primarily an amalgamation of these articles, drawn from "diverse pieces written in 1901 and 1902, some in heavyweight academic journals, but most in less exacting liberal and radical weeklies like the *Speaker*."[4] "Liberal" here refers to a current in British politics that emphasizes the importance of individual liberty.

These articles were written in London in the war's immediate aftermath. Deeply influenced by what he saw in Africa, Hobson solidified his convictions that imperialism represented a devastating ploy foisted on the many by the ultra-wealthy.[5] Most of those in Hobson's immediate circle were defined by their long-standing membership in London's "ethical societies." These were groups of left-leaning intellectuals who would meet and discuss socialist* politics, philosophy, and economics.

Author's Background
The most important defining historical features of *Imperialism* are "late-stage" British imperialism more generally—a period of time often called the "scramble for Africa"*—and the Boer War specifically. In the 1890s, European powers were preoccupied with grabbing land in Africa; the Cambridge historian John Lonsdale* compares it to a horse race: "steeplechases into the far interior," focusing on the "forcible conversion of existing European predominance" into direct political control.[6]

The result of this competition between long-standing imperial powers (Britain and France) and newcomers to the imperial project (Belgium, Germany, and Italy) created a massive shift in African politics. It has been pointed out that "in 1879, more than 90 percent of the [African] continent was ruled by Africans," but by 1900, while Hobson was composing *Imperialism*, "all but a tiny fraction of it was being governed by European powers."[7]

Hobson's connection to the European scramble for Africa came primarily through his involvement in the Boer War as a correspondent for the *Manchester Guardian*. The British journalist, author, and left-wing intellectual Nathaniel Mehr* writes: "The British had been successful in subduing the settler population and asserting their political and economic supremacy over South Africa's lucrative mining regions, but the campaign, with its imprisoning of rural women and children, was widely considered to have been something of an embarrassing debacle, prompting much earnest soul searching among Britain's political establishment."[8]

Long before those leaders searched their souls, however, Hobson searched for their political and economic motivations.

NOTES

1   John Hobson, *Imperialism: A Study* (Nottingham: Spokesman, 2011), 65.

2   Hobson, *Imperialism*, 85.

3   Jeremy Corbyn, foreword to *Imperialism: A Study*, by John Hobson (Nottingham: Spokesman, 2011), 7.

4   P. J. Cain, *Hobson and Imperialism: Radicalism, New Liberalism, and Finance: 1887–1938* (Oxford: Oxford University Press, 2002), 82.

5   Cain, *Hobson and Imperialism*, 92.

6   John Lonsdale, "The European Scramble and Conquest in African History," in *The Cambridge History of Africa*, vol. 6, *c. 1870—c. 1905*, ed. Roland Oliver and G. N. Sanderson (Cambridge: Cambridge University Press, 1985), 681.

7   Roland Oliver and Anthony Atmore, *Africa since 1800* (Cambridge: Cambridge University Press, 2005), 118.

8   Nathaniel Mehr, "Introduction," in *Imperialism: A Study*, by John Hobson (Nottingham: Spokesman, 2011), 15.

MODULE 2
ACADEMIC CONTEXT

KEY POINTS

- The academic field of political economy* is concerned with examining the nature of wealth, and how societies can be made prosperous.

- Although liberal* political economists (that is, thinkers on economic matters who favored individual liberty) such as Adam Smith* and Jeremy Bentham* believed imperialism* was costly in terms of wealth, those such as John Stuart Mill* believed the value came from "civilizing" savage lands.

- While Hobson believed markets were usually imperfect, he agreed with classical liberal thinkers that imperialism— the policy of seizing foreign territory, generally with some kind of profit in mind—was expensive and immoral.

The Work in its Context

John Hobson's *Imperialism: A Study* is a work of political economy: an academic tradition primarily concerned with, in the famous description of the English political philosopher John Stuart Mill, "the nature of Wealth, and the laws of its production and distribution: including, directly or remotely, the operation of all the causes by which the condition of mankind … is made prosperous or the reverse."[1]

Political economy, in other words, looks at the relationship between wealth and society, and how different ways of producing wealth can create more or less prosperity. One of the most important conclusions to draw from Mill's statement is that the field of political economy is immersed in philosophy and ideas of how to distribute and produce the most value. Thus it is a much "wider" discipline than simply politics or economics.

> ❝ In every department of human affairs Practice long precedes Science ... The conception, accordingly, of Political Economy as a branch of science is extremely modern; but the subject with which its enquiries are conversant has in all ages necessarily constituted one of the chief practical interests of mankind, and in some, a most unduly engrossing one. That subject is Wealth. ❞
>
> John Stuart Mill, *Principles of Political Economy*

Within the discipline, Hobson was profoundly influenced by the liberal tradition, which emphasized individual freedom and the idea that society could be made "rational." The tradition owes much to the influential English political theorist John Locke,* whose *Second Treatise of Government*, a foundational text for liberal thought, argued that government existed to protect private property.[2] Liberal political economists have a long history of criticizing imperialism; if government exists only to protect people's rights and property, then holding empires is surplus to requirements—and so, a waste of time and money.

Overview of the Field

Hobson was deeply influenced by broadly conceived ideas of liberalism as defined by its great thinkers (notably the Scottish economist Adam Smith, the English philosopher and social reformer Jeremy Bentham, and the English political philosopher John Stuart Mill).

Liberalism and imperialism had an uneasy relationship from the start. Smith highlighted the costly nature of imperial mercantilism* (roughly speaking, trade encouraged by government policy) in his seminal book *Wealth of Nations*, writing that while empire "[raises] up a nation of customers, who should be obliged to buy from the shops of our different producers ... the home consumers have been burdened with the expense of maintaining and defending that empire," much to their detriment.[3] Bentham wrote of imperialism's moral problems: "[Give] up your colonies," he urged European statesmen, in a 1793 pamphlet entitled *Emancipate Your Colonies*, "because you have no right to govern them, because they had rather not be governed by you."[4]

By contrast, Mill complicated the standard liberal position, arguing that imperialism should be seen as a relationship of mutual benefit between Britain and her domains. Like Hobson after him, Mill believed that England had a surplus of population and capital (roughly, money available to be invested) that needed an outlet abroad through empire. Unlike Hobson, however, Mill believed empire to be a good solution and claimed not only that England's empire extended English liberalism throughout the so-called "unoccupied" lands of the world, but also that "the uncivilized dependencies also benefitted from the order and security, the investment and trade England provided."[5]

Despite their differences, all these thinkers are concerned with the relationship between prosperity and morality. In many ways, the political economy argument against imperial policy has usually been that it is both valueless, being very expensive and without benefit, and immoral, in terms of rights. Mill's justification of imperialism still fits this schema—except he argues that the morality of "civilizing" imperial subjects justifies the idea.

Academic Influences

Hobson's liberal thinking dates to his days at Oxford University, where his association with the liberal thinker T. H. Green* shaped his own broadly defined position as a "new"* (or "social"*) liberal:[6] he believed, that is, that the state has a role in ensuring personal liberty, notably by ensuring economic social justice.

Green is most famous for discussing the difference between "negative" liberty—a freedom from restriction, such as freedom of speech—and "positive" liberty, which is all about being enabled (being taught to speak, for example).[7] This was an important distinction between "classical" and "new" liberalism: classical liberalism emphasized freedom from government interference (negative liberty), whereas new liberalism focused on the obligation of individuals to help one another.

P. J. Cain,* one of Hobson's contemporary critics, wrote that new liberalism emphasized the rights of the community, rather than the individual, considering the individual flawed. This led new liberals to reject the perfect market of Say's Law,* which held that production is the source of all demand—that is, a worker will buy products with his or her income, in turn encouraging production in other areas.

Instead, new liberals viewed the market "as divisive, exacerbating poverty and threatening social collapse," and therefore wanting active control by the government.[8] This view was also broadly shared by two further great nineteenth-century liberals—John Ruskin* and Richard Cobden*—who inspired Hobson to such an extent that he would write their biographies.

Cobden was among the first, most strident voices to insist that imperialism was bad for England, writing: "It is … an abiding conviction in my mind that we have entered upon an impossible and hopeless career in India."[9] Hobson took the standard liberal analysis of empire—that it is expensive and immoral—a step further by insisting that the imperial project was not just misplaced national fervor, but also the cynical plan of financiers* (people who profit from lending large sums of money to business ventures).

NOTES

1   John Stuart Mill, *Principles of Political Economy with Some of Their Applications to Social Philosophy* (London: Longmans, 1865), 1.

2   John Locke, *Second Treatise of Government*, ed. C. B. Macpherson (Indianapolis, IN: Hackett, 1980), 20.

3   Adam Smith, *An Inquiry into the Nature and Causes of the Wealth of Nations* (London: Digireads, 2009), 391.

4   Jeremy Bentham, quoted in Bernard Porter, *Critics of Empire: British Radicals and the Imperial Challenge* (London: I. B. Tauris, 2007), 8.

5   Eileen Sullivan, "Liberalism and Imperialism: J. S. Mill's Defence of the British Empire," *Journal of the History of Ideas* 44, no. 4 (1983): 607–9.

6   P. J. Cain, *Hobson and Imperialism: Radicalism, New Liberalism, and Finance: 1887–1938* (Oxford: Oxford University Press, 2002), 21.

7   T. H. Green, "Liberal Legislation and Freedom of Contract," in *The Political Theory of T. H. Green: Selected Writings*, ed. John R. Rodman (New York: Meredith, 1964), 44–5.

8   Cain, *Hobson and Imperialism*, 21.

9   Richard Cobden, quoted in Porter, *Critics of Empire*, 13.

MODULE 3
THE PROBLEM

KEY POINTS

- The book's core question is "What is the economic rationale behind imperial foreign policy?"

- The debate was not an academic debate so much as a public debate; both inside and out of politics, attempts were made to justify imperialism on commercial grounds ("trade follows the flag") and moral grounds ("we are obliged to civilize the savage").

- Hobson and his fellow liberals* rejected both these claims. Hobson's counterargument was founded on a very tight scientific theory.

Core Question

With Europe's frantic scramble for Africa,* many political economists asked the question "What is the economic rationale behind this imperialist* foreign policy?" The common explanation of imperialist economics was mercantilist:* described by the assertion that "trade follows the flag," the basic idea of mercantilism is that the imperial nation needs raw materials for its industrial production at home and, therefore, requires territory abroad for two reasons. First, those territories supply the materials needed to manufacture products (which might be anything from clothing and furniture to guns) in the home country; second, once they are manufactured, these items get shipped out for purchase in the same colonies that provided the required materials in the first place.

This point of view emphasizes that the most prosperous trade relations exist between a country and its own territories, meaning that

> ❝ This war [the Boer War] is a terrible disaster for everyone else in England and South Africa, but for the mine owners it means a large increase of profits from a more economical working of the mines, and from speculative operations. ❞
>
> John Hobson, *The War in South Africa*

imperialism is an economically sensible policy for the home country to follow.

Understandably, this idea had its critics. Many liberal thinkers, from Adam Smith* through Hobson, believed the mercantilism model was deeply flawed, and that imperialism was actually very expensive for Britain. The Boer War,* a conflict between the forces of the British Empire and the descendants of seventeenth-century Dutch settlers in what is today South Africa, represented a major moment for this question, and it is crucial to remember that Hobson had witnessed this debacle first hand. Hobson saw the apparent absurdity of imperialism, and his book attempted to understand why Britain might engage in such a mistaken venture. The wrongs committed in the name of the narrow interests of finance capitalism*—private profit made through private investment—were veiled in the discussion of a British struggle. Thus Hobson, among others, questioned imperial policy on both its economic and moral bases.

The Participants

The debate between supporters and detractors of imperialism, as far as Hobson was concerned, did not occur like one staged in modern academia through journals or at universities. This debate was highly public, fought in the press and between the members of political parties.

The press was split between a majority of pro-war papers. As one historian puts it, "London journalists tended to portray the Boers as primitive and backwards … They were often described in animal terms … whose defeat by the superior civilization of the British was an inevitable result of social Darwinism"*—that is, roughly, as proof of the victors' inherent superiority and "evolutionary" advancement.[1] The domestic battleground was one of extreme patriotism,* where the war's critics were caricatured as "pro-Boer" or "anti-British"; Hobson dismissed the character of the debate as "jingoistic"* (by which he meant patriotic to an aggressive degree). His experiences were collected in his book *The War in South Africa*.[2]

This was not a simple public debate, however. Hobson was a member of the Liberal Party,* a political party that sought the creation of a basic welfare state and a more secular society, and that valued individual freedom over conformity and tradition. But its members sitting in the British Parliament were divided on the imperial issue; those sympathetic to the Boers were united by a mutual condemnation of "the military methods used in the war as unnecessary and inhumane," notably the use of concentration camps,* but were not organized by any leadership. Their pro-war colleagues tended to overlook these issues because "Imperialism was the popular horse to ride."[3] And since these debates were fought in the political and not the academic arena, subtle compromises ensued. The origins of imperialism were not discussed; participants in the debate were interested in advancing dogmatic viewpoints, a humanitarian cause, or their own political careers.

The Contemporary Debate

Hobson's approach was quite different from that of his fellow Liberals in Parliament.

A radical* (that is, someone who argued for social reforms designed to further the aims of left-wing liberalism),* he rejected these common views of imperialism, arguing that it was both immoral and unnecessarily expensive. Hobson was far from the only radical critic of imperialism, however. And nor was he the only one to accuse financiers* of being its chief instigators. Hobson's friend, the radical Scottish journalist J. M. Robertson,* wrote, for example: "The primary object [of imperialism] is not to buy, but to sell, and receive goods in return to sell again; all to the end of heaping up more capital for investment."[4] Such attacks further entrenched anti-imperialism as a liberal cause. Yet what distinguished Hobson, in part, was his increased focus on finance capitalism. While many of Hobson's contemporaries (Robertson among them) argued that industry was central to imperialism, Hobson pointed to a particular group of people as being primarily responsible.[5]

Hobson, then, did not simply follow the classical liberals,* who were sympathetic to free trade and objected to imperialism on moral grounds alone, or follow the new liberals,* for whom intervention in the market was a moral position, in simply pointing the finger at the financiers' antisocial saving behavior as encouraging the imperial project.

Instead, he crafted a social scientific theory with testable conclusions that directly connected investment-based capitalism and imperialism—a vital contribution to the arguments of the anti-imperialist cause.

NOTES

1   Kenneth Morgan, "The Boer War and the Media," *Twentieth Century British History* 13, no. 1 (2002): 5.

2   John Hobson, *The War in South Africa: Its Causes and Effects* (London: James Nisbet and Co. Ltd, 1900), 228.

3   John Auld, "The Liberal Pro-Boers," *Journal of British Studies* 14, no. 2 (1975): 93–4.

4   J. M. Robertson, *Patriotism and Empire* (London: Grant Richards, 1900), 172.

5   Peter Cain, "Radicalism, Gladstone and the Liberal Critique of Disraelian 'Imperialism,'" in *Victorian Visions of Global Order: Empire and International Relations in Nineteenth-Century Political Thought*, ed. Duncan Bell (Cambridge: Cambridge University Press, 2007), 226.

MODULE 4
THE AUTHOR'S CONTRIBUTION

KEY POINTS

- Hobson believed imperialism* was the direct result of finance capitalism*—that is, private investment made for the sake of private profit—and that inequality at home led to imperialism abroad.

- *Imperialism* sought to discredit claims that imperialism was profitable, while advancing the argument that it was an inevitable consequence of inequality.

- This argument was based on the theory of "underconsumption,"* according to which an economy will stagnate if there is not enough demand for products or services.

Author's Aims

John Hobson intended *Imperialism: A Study* to stand out from similar works by delivering a particularly devastating criticism of British imperial policy as a scheme of the ultra-wealthy financier* class. Imperialism, in other words, was a consequence of capitalism.

Hobson believed that imperialism resulted from domestic economic policy;[1] his goal was to provide an airtight, scientific theory that explained why massive inequalities in Britain created imperial policy abroad. He believed such a policy was in the interest of a few people of elite status—"financiers" who had accumulated so much capital that they could no longer profitably invest in Britain and wanted their investments abroad (such as gold mines and railroads) secured by military force.

Hobson intended his work to advocate for a policy change away from imperialism—which he saw as signifying the capture of the

> ❝ It is idle to attack Imperialism or Militarism* as political expedients or policies unless the axe is laid at the economic root of the tree, and the classes for whose interest Imperialism works are shorn of the surplus revenues which seek this outlet. ❞
>
> John Hobson, *Imperialism: A Study*

government by these financiers—toward social reform that included progressive taxation* (according to which taxation and earnings are linked), an increased minimum wage, and domestic redistribution programs to keep excess capital (profits, available for investment) at home, in the hands of consumers as wages.[2] Importantly, Hobson sought to arouse more than the British public's sense of decency (though he certainly argued against imperialism's immorality). He hoped to show how wealthy capitalists had defrauded them, and how it was in their best interests to reject imperialism.

Approach

To win over his readers, Hobson did more than argue against the economic rationale of imperialism, or implicate financiers for promoting a policy that hurt everyone else. *Imperialism* is distinctive because Hobson's ideas combine to connect domestic wealth inequality in Britain with imperialist policy abroad, showing how one is the direct cause of the other. His theory is valuable because it does not just moralize, but generates testable predictions. That is to say, Hobson's theory predicts that a class of finance capitalists living in a state will eventually cause that state to pursue imperialist policy—it is merely a matter of when.

This very bold forecast was one of the principal factors that served to undermine the success of Hobson's theory.

Hobson built his opinions on an economic theory he proposed in *The Physiology of Industry* (1889), a book he wrote with the businessman Albert Mummery.* This theory was "underconsumptionism."

Whereas orthodox economics held that production and consumption always matched each other, Hobson believed this was a skewed view. "If a tendency to distribute income or consuming power according to needs were operative," Hobson wrote, "it is evident that consumption would ride with every rise of producing power." But this was not true; increased production did not match increased consumption, as finance capitalists* had amassed and retained so much wealth that most consumers lacked the means to do much purchasing. As a result of the underconsumption that followed, financiers sought productive use of their capital abroad.[3] They needed an empire to put their money to work in generating profit.

Contribution in Context
Hobson first linked imperial policy and underconsumption in his 1898 paper "Free Trade and Foreign Policy," in which he wrote: "Though a potential market exists within the United Kingdom for all 'goods' produced by the nation, there is not an 'effective' demand."[4]

Here, he is describing what occurs when the consumer has the desire to acquire goods but oversaving capitalists thwart his or her ability to spend, keeping money out of circulation, tied up in their enormous stockpiles.

These wealthy people "have not the desire," since "their material needs" would be satisfied with just a fraction of their money, while those "who have the desire have not the power."[5] In other words, wealthy people have more money than could possibly be useful to fulfill even their most lavish desires, while the poor have no way of getting enough to satisfy their basic needs because of an economic imbalance.

"Saving," Hobson and Mummery wrote in their *Physiology of Industry*, "increases the existing aggregate of capital, [but] simultaneously reduces the quantity of utilities and conveniences consumed." Any "excess" of saving, then, places too much capital in the hands of a few capitalists. This both reduces the value of capital and deprives ordinary people of access to money, preventing them from spending.[6]

NOTES

1   John Hobson, *Imperialism: A Study* (Nottingham: Spokesman, 2011), 112.

2   Hobson, *Imperialism*, 108.

3   Hobson, *Imperialism*, 105.

4   John Hobson, "Free Trade and Foreign Policy," quoted in John D. Cunningham Wood and Robert D. Wood, *John A. Hobson: Critical Assessments of Leading Economists* (London: Routledge, 2003), xxxv.

5   Hobson, quoted in Wood and Wood, *John A. Hobson*, xxxv.

6   Albert Mummery and John Hobson, *The Physiology of Industry; Being an Exposure of Certain Fallacies in Existing Theories of Economics* (London: John Murray, 1889), vi–vii.

SECTION 2
IDEAS

MODULE 5
MAIN IDEAS

KEY POINTS

- Hobson's key themes are the political influence of the wealthy, the consequences of the economic stagnation caused by "underconsumption,"* and the social reform that was to solve these problems.

- Hobson's core argument is that consumption and production are not always in equilibrium, as finance capitalism* leads to underconsumption that throws off the balance between the two; finance capitalists exploit this imbalance to make and secure capital investments abroad; and imperialism* can be prevented with "social reform."

- Hobson's argument suffers from poor organization and a loose definition of the "financiers"* who are so important to his theory.

Key Themes

John Hobson's 1902 book, *Imperialism: A Study*, rests on a provocative overarching idea: the power of special interest groups—in this case, finance capitalists—to promote an imperialist policy in Britain. For Hobson, the wealthy finance capitalist is the "governor of the Imperial engine," because he possesses "those qualities of concentration and clear-sighted calculation which are needed to set Imperialism to work [in his favor]."[1]

This conclusion rests on a number of supporting arguments, including Hobson's theory of underconsumption, which consists of three sequential points:

- Excessive saving by the wealthy causes an oversupply of capital in industrial economies (that is, roughly, if the wealthy save rather than invest or spend, their money is tied up unproductively).

> ❝ It is not industrial progress that demands the opening up of new markets and areas of investment, but mal-distribution of consuming power which prevents the absorption of commodities and capital within the country. ❞
>
> John Hobson, *Imperialism: A Study*

- This in turn creates a strong incentive for the wealthy to export that capital.
- This goal of exporting capital encourages them to influence foreign policy.

"Social reform," Hobson believed, was the key to ending imperialism; an equitable distribution of wealth would end the inequality produced by underconsumption and remove the incentive to seize lands abroad.

Hobson's argument assumes that although people are rational, inasmuch as they want to do what is best for themselves, they are fallible, because they can be tricked about what is actually best. This belief is core to his social liberalism*—a political philosophy founded on the idea that governments need to redistribute resources through social reform to ensure a positive outcome for all.

Exploring the Ideas

The most important idea in Hobson's book is that finance capitalism does not just encourage imperialism, it *causes* imperialism: "Imperialism is the endeavor of the great controllers of industry to broaden the channel for the flow of their surplus wealth by seeking foreign markets and foreign investments to take off the goods and capital they cannot sell or use at home."[2]

The root cause of this state of affairs, for Hobson, is "the mal-distribution of capital within the country. The oversaving [of capital by the financier class] which is the economic root of Imperialism is found to consist of rents, monopoly profits, and other unearned or excessive elements of income."[3]

More importantly, this hoarded capital finds no use at home; though it exists in profound abundance, it largely rests outside the hands of actual consumers. Hobson believes that the need to "fight for foreign markets or foreign areas of investment" would disappear if the ultra-wealthy were not allowed to accumulate so much capital in the first place.[4]

This idea was notable because of the way it complicated Say's Law.* Named after the liberal* French economist Jean-Baptiste Say,* this law states that a paid producer of goods then purchases the production of others in a continuous economic cycle. But as Hobson saw it, Say's Law could be contravened by oversaving; government intervention would then be needed to maintain equilibrium between consumption and production as a natural, orderly state of economic affairs.

Hobson's solution to the problem, then, is not to abandon imperialism: this would treat the symptom rather than the disease. Rather, Hobson advocated abandoning unregulated capitalism that allowed imperialism to arise in the first place. His solution was the redistribution of wealth through social programs, or social reform; through social reform, domestic inequality that leads to Britain's capital oversupply would be solved, and the financier class's massive incentive to encourage imperialism would be dismantled. Trade unions* (associations of laborers formed to protect the interests of working people) and socialism* (very roughly, a political philosophy founded on the idea that the government should intervene in the free market in order to protect society by ensuring a reasonably equitable distribution of wealth), both engines of social reform, "are thus the natural enemies of Imperialism, for they take away from the 'imperialist' classes the surplus incomes which form the economic stimulus of Imperialism."[5] In other words, Britain's foreign policy can only become ethical by confronting the imperialist leanings created by its domestic economy.

Language and Expression

A dominant theme—that oversaving by financiers leads them to advance their interests via imperialism—is generally expressed well in the first part of the book. Hobson presents his data clearly, often in table form, before discussing them and does not break off onto tangents. Despite this, it could be argued that the communication of the idea breaks down in two ways.

First, Hobson's overall theory rests on an assumption that he fails to prove or explore thoroughly: that the financier class possesses a near-perfect ability to direct "the patriotic forces" generated by "politicians, soldiers, philanthropists, and traders" into an imperialist policy that does not serve the interests of the people.[6] Hobson never makes clear, however, how these rich figures wield such control over the government.

Second, the latter half of the book leaves readers unclear as to whether financiers lead the imperialist drive, or follow the winds of foreign political expansion. Either they brandish "those qualities of concentration and clear-sighted calculation which are needed to set Imperialism to work," or "they simply and instinctively attach to themselves any strong, genuine elevated feeling … and utilize it for their ends."[7] The apparently contradictory nature of Hobson's argument makes it difficult for the reader to decide which strategy dominates.

Hobson's key idea suffers because he treats the financier class as a kind of analytical dumping ground in his attempt to link causes and effects: they are not clearly enough defined and their powers are seemingly limitless. This problem has led critics to dismiss Hobson's work as a "conspiracy theory."[8]

NOTES

1   John Hobson, *Imperialism: A Study* (Nottingham: Spokesman, 2011), 88.

2   Hobson, *Imperialism*, 106.

3   Hobson, *Imperialism*, 107.

4   Hobson, *Imperialism*, 107.

5   Hobson, *Imperialism*, 110.

6   Hobson, *Imperialism*, 88.

7   Hobson, *Imperialism*, 88, 191.

8   Nathaniel Mehr, "Introduction," in John Hobson, *Imperialism: A Study* (Nottingham: Spokesman, 2011), 29.

MODULE 6
SECONDARY IDEAS

KEY POINTS

- Hobson's moral argument against imperialism* is based on a distinction between "imperialism," which is exploitative, and "colonialism,"* which expands the nation; he also cautions against imperialism's threat to democracy at home.

- Hobson's secondary arguments, which refute the idea that imperialism is a moral good, are unconcerned with the economic effects of imperialism; that is another debate.

- Hobson's book is being re-examined in terms of capitalist institutions protecting themselves by eradicating alternatives around the world.

Other Ideas

The thrust of Hobson's main argument—that inequality at home leads to imperialism abroad—is supported by his more philosophical sub-argument. Hobson concerned himself with refuting the idea that imperialism was a beneficial international project and warned of the effects that excessive militarism*—a social tendency toward the exercise of military action, or a society reflecting a military model—would have on the British domestic situation. More imperialism abroad, he maintained, meant less liberal* democracy at home.

And while "imperialism" and "colonialism"* might seem to be words with identical meanings, Hobson draws an important distinction between the two by outlining the differences between the extension of national rights and the imposition of authority. Hobson defines nationalism* as "the establishment of a political community on the basis of nationality," and so colonialism merely extends that

> **❝** There exists an absolute antagonism between the activity of the good citizen and that of the soldier. The end of the soldier is not, as is sometimes falsely said, to die for his country, it is to kill for his country. **❞**
>
> John Hobson, *Imperialism: A Study*

community—and the nation—through movement of citizens with full political rights to unpopulated lands. Imperialism, on the other hand, occurs "when a nation advances beyond the limits of nationality," and instead of governing fellow citizens with full rights, despotically possesses and exploits territory and people.[1]

Understanding the dissimilarities between "colonialism" and "imperialism" is crucial to understanding Hobson's moral argument about how British international projects ought to operate.

Exploring the Ideas

At a time when the "mission of civilization" was often touted as the moral purpose of imperialism, Hobson refuted this idea as part of his international argument. "In considering the ethics and politics of [imperial] interference," he wrote, "we must not be bluffed or blinded by critics who fasten on the palpable dishonesty of many practices of the gospel of the 'dignity of labour' and the 'mission of civilization.'"[2] The only legitimate interference with "lower races," Hobson believed, should work to bring them up to a state of rational self-government, and not exploit them in the interest of the civilizing country.[3]

This idea of imperialism as education to benefit the colonized dated back to the English liberal philosopher John Stuart Mill,* who saw four stages of societal development. These began with savagery and progressed to slavery and barbarism, "which is characterized, above all, by 'mental' shortcomings … and 'positive defects of national character' making representative government impossible"; this was finally followed by modern liberal statehood.[4] He believed more developed nations must encourage the growth of those that lagged behind them.

Hobson, however, considered Mill's four steps as a moral cover for the profitable exploitation of the so-called "lower races," and that it would "preclude the genuine sympathy essential to the operation of the best civilizing influences."[5]

He also made a domestic argument against imperialism, charging that it promoted militarism and eroded democracy. "So far," Hobson wrote, "I have regarded the issue on its narrowly economic side. Far more important are the political implications of militarism [that] strike at the very root of popular liberty and the ordinary civic virtues."[6] Thus liberalism and militarism exist as opposite principles, "the one making for the evolution of the good citizen, the other for the evolution of the good soldier."[7]

In other words, good citizens have a social, cooperative attitude, while good soldiers have a dictatorial, forceful one. Hobson believes that when a soldier enters government, he will be more likely to command and oppress. Yet this critique of the imperial project as counter to liberalism was not original to Hobson. It had its origins among mid-nineteenth-century liberals such as the British statesman Richard Cobden,* who wrote: "It may seem Utopian, but I don't feel sympathy for a great nation, or for those who desire greatness of a people by vast extension of empire. What I like to see is the growth, development, and elevation of the individual man."[8]

Overlooked

The second part of Hobson's book focuses on the political concerns surrounding imperialism and is less often discussed than the first, which examines the economics of imperialism. The economic historian Lars Magnusson,* however, believes that increased focus on the neglected second part of the book does much to revitalize

Hobson's theory. Most interpreters and critics of Hobson throughout the twentieth century focused only on his narrow economic explanation of imperialism, and it is popular to regard *Imperialism* as a prototype* for the book *Imperialism is the Highest Form of Capitalism*, a Marxist* analysis by the Russian revolutionary leader Vladimir Lenin.*

Magnusson, however, believes that economic explanations must always be set in the context of political ones, and that doing so shows Hobson as much more than a prototypical Lenin. He maintains that Hobson's real picture of "aggressive Imperialism after 1870" relied on "the emergence of theories of [social Darwinism],* including race theories, as well as the revival of increased nationalism and misguided patriotism."*9

In other words, Magnusson contends that a proper reading of Hobson gives as much weight to the second section of *Imperialism* as the first, and sees the economic explanation as only one part of a much more intricate theory that embraces history, politics, ideology, and economics.

Magnusson asserts that seeing Hobson in this way has major implications for how to perceive the entire book. For him, *Imperialism* "should rather be regarded as a precursor of modern institutional economics"*—that is, the study of how institutions and ideas shape economic behavior—"than merely a prototype of defunct Leninist* theory of Imperialism."*10

Magnusson also holds that the role of finance capitalists* in Hobson's theory is, in fact, relatively restricted and that his theory of imperialism should be seen as more similar to that of the American economist Thorstein Veblen.* "Imperialism," Veblen believed, "is dynastic politics under a new name, carried on for the benefit of absentee owners instead of absentee princes."11 In the context of Magnusson's reappraisal, a striking similarity emerges between the ideas of Hobson and Veblen. For Hobson, institutions such as patriotism and racism play a pivotal, rather than a secondary, role, while Veblen relies on "patriotism … as an additional explanatory variable [in] his theory of capitalism including its international dimension, imperialism."[12]

NOTES

1   John Hobson, *Imperialism: A Study* (Nottingham: Spokesman, 2011), 45–8.

2   Hobson, *Imperialism*, 213.

3   Hobson, *Imperialism*, 214.

4   Beate Jahn, "Kant, Mill, and Illiberal Legacies in International Affairs," *International Organization* 59, no. 1 (2005): 194.

5   Hobson, *Imperialism*, 250.

6   Hobson, *Imperialism*, 142.

7   Hobson, *Imperialism*, 144.

8   Richard Cobden, quoted in Bernard Porter, *Critics of Empire: British Radicals and the Imperial Challenge* (London: I. B. Tauris, 2007), 14.

9   Lars Magnusson, "Hobson and Imperialism: An Appraisal," in *J. A. Hobson after Fifty Years*, ed. John Pheby (London: Macmillan, 1994), 156.

10 Magnusson, "Hobson and Imperialism," 160.

11 Thorstein Veblen, *Absentee Ownership and Business Enterprise in Recent Times* (New York: Kelley, 1964), 35.

12 Stephen Edgell and Jules Townshend, "John Hobson, Thorstein Veblen, and the Phenomenon of Imperialism: Finance Capital, Patriotism, and War," *American Journal of Economics and Sociology* 51, no. 4 (1992): 412.

MODULE 7
ACHIEVEMENT

KEY POINTS

- Although Hobson's "scientific" theory of imperialism*
  itself did not have lasting impact, the general thrust of his
  thought has retained importance.

- Imperialism remained a force in the twentieth century,
  and Hobson remained relevant to the study of this
  phenomenon.

- *Imperialism* maintains a complicated relationship with
  issues of race: Hobson implicated Jewish people in
  perpetrating imperialism.

Assessing the Argument

While *Imperialism: A Study* retains a great deal of importance, John
Hobson did not quite accomplish his key goal of establishing a direct
causal chain between inequality and imperialism. Hobson is prone to
"conceptual slippage," meaning that his analysis of imperialism appears
contradictory; certain concepts become narrower and broader as he
writes. One of the best examples of this slippage involves Hobson's
idea of capitalists* who act as the governing force of imperialism, and
whether they believe their own jingoism* (that is, aggressive love of
one's country).

In the first part of the book, imperialists are cynical financiers,*
motivated only by their investment needs as they seek to manipulate a
credulous Britain into pursuing a destructive imperialist policy.[1] Later
in the book, however, when discussing the psychological power of
imperialism, Hobson admits a good deal more emotion and
patriotism* to the financier class: "Imperialist politicians, soldiers, or

> 66 One must, however, insist again that Hobson's lasting contribution is his psychological analysis of imperialism. He was at his best in laying bare the roots of man's infinite capacity for self-deception, for man naturally seeks some ethical underpinnings for his approval of policies he would ordinarily condemn at home. 99
>
> Harvey Mitchell, "Hobson Revisited," *Journal of the History of Ideas*

company directors who push a forward policy by portraying the cruelties of the African slave raids … do not deliberately and consciously work up these motives in order to incite the British public. They simply and instinctively attach to themselves any strong, genuine elevated feeling … and utilize it for their ends."[2]

If Hobson did not realize his goal of providing a universal discrediting of imperial policy, it is because of this conceptual slippage. Although the "financier class" is of critical importance to his theory, his definition of that class changes as his argument develops; this may, however, be a consequence of the fact that *Imperialism* was not composed as a single work, but was produced from a number of cobbled-together papers.

Achievement in Context

In his eagerness to create a universally applicable "theory" of imperialism akin to science, Hobson may have overstated his case. He wrote that maldistribution of wealth in one country leads to global imperialism as fire leads to smoke, but in reality it is difficult to make these absolute arguments in the complex realm of society. This explains in large part why his work met with a lukewarm reception among his fellow liberals* and was virtually ignored by the general public early on. More sympathetic interest in Hobson's theory arose later—first in the Marxism* of the Russian communist leader Vladimir Lenin* and later in the 1960s, as interest in the study of imperialism grew in the context of the Cold War* (a 44–year period of tension between the United States, the Soviet Union,* and the nations aligned around them).

The focus of imperialism shifted from Britain to America and, during the Cold War, the Soviet Union. Renewed interest in the study of imperialism, as Michael Barratt Brown* wrote in the introduction to *The Economics of Imperialism*, "certainly reflects widespread dissatisfaction with narrowly political explanations [of imperial activity], in terms of 'defending the free world' or 'rescuing the achievements of communism,'* respectively, for what the United States has been doing in the Caribbean and Southeast Asia and the Soviet Union in Eastern Europe."[3]

Limitations

Imperialism has endured criticisms of anti-Semitism* (anti-Jewish sentiment) and Eurocentrism* (a world view that prioritizes the pre-eminence and assumptions of Europe and European people).

The former comes from Hobson's line that the financier class in supposed control of imperial policy consists mainly of "men of a single and peculiar [Jewish] race, who have behind them many centuries of financial experience."[4] Anti-Semitism was common in Hobson's political circles, and he was ultimately seen as the victim of a popular stereotype that located "responsibility for the [Boer] War* … [in] the unworthy motives of Jewish financiers."[5]

While he indicted Jews as responsible for capitalism,* this did not form a major part of his argument, and this belief has not changed the way Hobson is seen today. His more extended treatment of the "lower races" as children needing guidance, however, is much more controversial in a modern context. The conclusion that white interference in non-white society is necessary as a "civilizing mission" forms the basis for Hobson's justification of a "benign" or "sane" imperialism.[6]

This picture poses problems, as the Canadian international relations professor David Long* points out. First, Hobson fails to recognize that these societies were perfectly able to govern themselves without white interference. And second, Hobson's problem with imperialism is "not with [the] notion of control over subject peoples but rather the competition among the Western nations for control, that is, as bad fathers or bad teachers."[7] This vein of criticism has made Hobson's call for "sane" imperialism less valid, and reveals that his vision of capitalism, even if inspired by perceived injustice, lacked pinpoint focus.

NOTES

1   John Hobson, *Imperialism: A Study* (Nottingham: Spokesman, 2011), 86.

2   Hobson, *Imperialism*, 191.

3   Michael Barratt Brown, *The Economics of Imperialism* (London: Penguin, 1974), 17–18.

4   Hobson, *Imperialism*, 86.

5   Harvey Mitchell, "Hobson Revisited," *Journal of the History of Ideas* 26, no. 3 (1965): 400.

6   Hobson, *Imperialism,* 216.

7   David Long, "Paternalism and the Internationalization of Imperialism: J. A. Hobson on the International Government of the 'Lower Races,'" in *Imperialism and Internationalism in the Discipline of International Relations*, ed. David Long and Brian Schmidt (Albany: University of New York Press, 2005), 87.

MODULE 8
PLACE IN THE AUTHOR'S WORK

KEY POINTS

- Hobson's main focus was on tying economic theories to political outcomes, though he focused mostly on politics later in life.
- Hobson's later work ignored the economic justifications of imperialism* and concentrated more on human nature.
- Hobson's work was dismissed in his lifetime; even the economist John Maynard Keynes,* who admired Hobson, found his writing style confusing and the quality variable.

Positioning

John Hobson's *Imperialism: A Study* came about in the midst of an extremely prolific career. While it is usually (though not exclusively) lauded as his most enduring work of importance, it was neither his first major treatise on economics, nor his first on imperialism.

Hobson's first major work, co-written with British businessman Albert Mummery* in 1889, was *The Physiology of Industry*, where he outlined the underconsumption theory* that would provide the theme for most of his subsequent work. *Imperialism* was not Hobson's first anti-imperialist work. His 1898 article "Free Trade and Foreign Policy" outlined his theory of economic imperialism, tying underconsumption theory to imperial expansion, and proposing domestic reform as a peaceful, desirable alternative. In the article, he drew a sharp distinction between imperialism and the "internal social and industrial reforms" required to achieve an even distribution of wealth.[1] Hobson would go on to provide evidence for this theory in *Imperialism*.

> **"** By enlisting my combative instincts in defence of
> my heretical views of capitalism as the source of unjust
> distribution, oversaving, and an economic impulsion
> to adventurous imperialism, it led me for a time to an
> excessive and too simple advocacy of the economic
> determination of history. **"**
>
> John Hobson, *Confessions of an Economic Heretic*

He later moderated his extreme position, writing in his autobiography, *Confessions of an Economic Heretic*, that "by enlisting my combative instincts in defence of my heretical views of capitalism as a source of unjust distribution, oversaving, and an economic impulsion to adventurous imperialism, it led me for a time to an excessive and too simple advocacy of the economic determination of history."[2] In this later period of Hobson's life—*Heretic* was published two years before his death in 1940—he adopted a much more general view of imperialism: he believed it resulted from the natural acquisitiveness and assertiveness of human beings rather than any particular economic system.

Integration

While largely focused on the theme of underconsumption and concerned with imperial expansion, Hobson's body of work was not necessarily unified. For example, Hobson's very earliest work on imperialism was not anti-imperialist, and he did not remain convinced of his own conclusions as his career continued past *Imperialism*. This is evident in his 1911 article "An Economic Interpretation of Investment," where he softened his previous position, writing that the international character of many investment cartels removes the "temptation or ... ability" of financiers* to manipulate states into imperial policies.[3]

In the wake of World War I,* however, Hobson was filled with renewed pessimism as to whether economic interdependence could supplant militarism* (the belief that a nation's aims can be achieved by military action) in developed nations. This led him first to reduce the role of financiers and increase the role of politicians in promoting foreign militarism in his 1917 book *Democracy after the War.* Then, in his 1926 book *Free Thought in the Social Sciences*, he concluded that "Imperialism is mainly the expression of two dominant human instincts, self-assertion and acquisitiveness."[4] But *Free Thought* also represents a widening of Hobson's scope of inquiry as he considers the nature of the social sciences themselves—and of man in society—rather than a particular social phenomenon.

Now more interested in how psychology can be folded into the field of political economy, Hobson identifies human nature as the independent cause of imperialism, and explains that his original economic explanation only masked this fact. From this time on, he became more interested in social theories in general, rather than theories of any narrow phenomenon. Still, a single characteristic unites all of Hobson's work: his preoccupation with how government intervention, and the redistribution of wealth in particular, can improve the lives of all.

Significance

Hobson's body of work has had mixed fortunes overall; outside "small coteries of friends, admirers, and like-minded social critics," he did not have a wide impact on political thought until some years later.[5] Yet subsequent thinkers, including the Russian leader Vladimir Lenin* and the English economist John Maynard Keynes,* have credited Hobson as a direct inspiration. But he was also a flawed one, as Keynes noted when he assessed the mixed power of Hobson's body of work in 1914: "One comes to a new book by Mr. Hobson with mixed feelings," he wrote, "in hope of stimulating ideas and some fruitful criticisms of orthodoxy from an independent and individual standpoint, but expectant of much sophistry, misunderstanding, and perverse thought."[6]

This general observation reflects the view of Hobson's argument in *Imperialism* as profoundly insightful but ultimately flawed. Yet because of its insight, *Imperialism* has enjoyed continued influence around the world, especially when the Cold War* ignited an international power struggle between the United States and the Soviet Union.* Once again, critics of empire referred back to Hobson to wonder whether the international escapades of the two superpowers were actually driven by narrow economic interests.

Those critics were not necessarily "Hobsonites," however, as they did not share Hobson's theory and its strong claims, sharing instead his general suspicion of wealthy countries pursuing international military projects.

NOTES

1   John Hobson, quoted in P. J. Cain, *Hobson and Imperialism: Radicalism, New Liberalism, and Finance: 1887–1938* (Oxford: Oxford University Press, 2002), 75.

2   John Hobson, *Confessions of an Economic Heretic* (Hassocks: Harvester Press, 1976), 63.

3   John Hobson, quoted in Michael Schneider, *J. A. Hobson* (London: Macmillan, 1996), 102.

4   Schneider, *J. A. Hobson*, 103.

5   Michael Freeden, *Reappraising J. A. Hobson* (London: Unwin Hyman, 1990), 3.

6   John Maynard Keynes, "Review of *Gold, Prices, and Wages*," *Economic Journal* 23 (1913): 393.

SECTION 3
IMPACT

MODULE 9
THE FIRST RESPONSES

KEY POINTS

- *Imperialism*, upon publication, was either ignored or dismissed for failing to prove its "conspiracy theory" of perfect control by financiers.*

- Hobson responded by trying to tie his "conspiracy theory" to real figures—exaggerating the role of Cecil Rhodes,* for example.

- *Imperialism* was never popular for its theory, but rather for its argument that imperial policy was irrational. When the Cold War* renewed debate about imperial policy, *Imperialism* was once again part of the conversation.

Criticism

Imperialism:A Study had little immediate impact outside the immediate circle of John Hobson's fellow radicals.* As a result, the first criticisms Hobson endured did not come from conservatives or pro-imperialists, but from fellow liberals* who believed he overstated his case. "Even amongst some of the Liberals and Radicals who agreed with Hobson," writes the British history professor P. J. Cain,* *Imperialism* was ignored because it was seen to "absurdly overstate" the evils of imperialism.*[1]

The English author Norman Angell,* writing under the pseudonym Ralph Lane, was one of Hobson's more prominent critics. He pointed out that Hobson imbued the financier class with a near-superhuman ability to influence policy—and with near-inhuman detachment. "The intensity of feeling," Angell wrote, "which embraced … the whole nation—a feeling which in every characteristic was non-rational—precludes the idea that it had its origins or is mainly

> ❝ Hobson's sinister capitalists and their 'parasites' were nothing more than a hypothesis, a *deus ex machina*, to balance an equation between the assumed rationality of mankind and the unreasonableness of imperial policies: and the book was a plea for a return to a sane standard of values. His mistake, then, was to think that the equation needed such artificial adjustment. ❞
>
> D. K. Fieldhouse, "*Imperialism*: An Historiographical Revision," *Economic History Review*

animated by a limited clique whose motives are intensely rationalistic."[2]

This criticism of the conspiracy theory damaged Hobson's case, and its ill-defined stereotype of an all-powerful financier class would plague it. Even *Imperialism*'s most favorable newspaper review was far from flattering. The *Edinburgh Review* agreed with Angell that it was preposterous to suppose that British policy was dictated by "self interested groups of financiers and millionaires," and that these exaggerations concealed from readers the underlying power and appeal of its argument against imperial policy.[3]

Responses

Though Hobson reissued *Imperialism* in 1905, he altered the text very little. The British historian P. J. Cain gives a list of his alterations: "Hobson tried to strengthen his claims about the weak association between foreign trade growth and recent Imperial expansion," and he reclassified South Africa as a "tropical" (meaning ñon-white) territory as opposed to a "white-settled" one (akin to Australia or Canada). Ultimately, though, he left his core argument largely unaltered.[4]

While not a direct response to his critics, Hobson reissued his first major work, *The Evolution of Modern Capitalism*, in 1906, just a year after reissuing *Imperialism*. In this printing of *Capitalism*, Hobson wrote a new chapter laying out the general power of the financier class in a more concrete way than *Imperialism* did, focusing on the British tycoon and statesman Cecil Rhodes: "The most distinctive feature of South African finance has been the skilled use which the financiers have made of political machinery to assist them in improving and marketing investments. The actual lands which form the material basis of industrial and speculative exploitation … have in each case involved in their acquisition the application of a medley of non-economic forces, legal treachery … and diplomatic coercion."[5]

While Hobson pointed to the success of the financiers, and their propensity to fiddle in politics, he still did not fix the break in his line between financial capitalism and imperialism. And so the question remained: how, specifically, do financiers wield such comprehensive power to write policy?

Conflict and Consensus

Critical debate around *Imperialism* was largely unproductive, and nothing resembling a fruitful academic discourse emerged until later in the twentieth century. By this time, the conspiracy elements of Hobson's theory were dropped in favor of a more complex set of relationships between state and finance interests.

Of the criticisms Hobson endured in the twentieth century, the one from the historian D. K. Fieldhouse,* a specialist in the British Empire, was the most thorough. "Hobson's own claim to importance and originality lies simply in his having introduced British, and subsequently world, opinion to accept his special definition of the word Imperialism."[6] This definition held that imperialism was a kind of degenerate, exploitative endeavor in the narrow capitalist* interests of the imperialist state. Fieldhouse believed that Hobson's economic theory of imperialism, and its focus on finance capitalists,* was "a pamphlet for the times, rather than a serious study of the subject …

[owing] much of its success to the fact that it expressed a current idea with peculiar clarity, force, and conviction."[7]

Ultimately, Fieldhouse found Hobson's economic theory unsound because it failed to explain capital export properly: "Detailed investigations have shown that the alleged needs of the European investor ... to find outlets for his surplus capital had little or nothing to do with the division of Africa and the Pacific between the European powers." Moreover, imperial expansion after 1870 resulted from the need to protect existing possessions, and "on the economic side," motivations were largely unchanged.[8]

Yet having established these points, Fieldhouse believes that Hobson's analysis had one major valuable aspect: it asserted that imperialism was largely irrational. But since Hobson could not accept this at face value, he had to invent a conspiracy of financiers for whom it was rational—figures who Fieldhouse believed were "a hypothesis ... to balance an equation between the assumed rationality of mankind and the unreasonableness of imperial policies."[9]

NOTES

1   P. J. Cain, *Hobson and Imperialism: Radicalism, New Liberalism, and Finance: 1887–1938* (Oxford: Oxford University Press, 2002), 163–4.

2   Norman Angell, quoted in Cain, *Hobson and Imperialism*, 118–19.

3   Timo Särkkä, *Hobson's Imperialism: A Study in Late Victorian Political Thought* (Jyväskylä: University of Jyväskylä, 2009), 166.

4   Cain, *Hobson and Imperialism*, 171–2.

5   John Hobson, *The Evolution of Modern Capitalism* (London: The Walter Scott Publishing Company, 1906), 266.

6   D. K. Fieldhouse, "Imperialism: An Historiographical Revision," *Economic History Review* 14, no. 2 (1961): 187.

7   Fieldhouse, "Imperialism," 189.

8   Fieldhouse, "Imperialism," 213.

9   Fieldhouse, "Imperialism," 214.

MODULE 10
THE EVOLVING DEBATE

KEY POINTS

- Hobson's *Imperialism* helped inaugurate debates on the relationship between economic interests at home and political aggression abroad, and dismissed arguments about trade and racial ethics.

- Marxist* thinkers such as Vladimir Lenin* and the Polish German activist Rosa Luxemburg* took Hobson's ideas and extended them to call for revolution rather than reform; modern Marxist thinkers such as Ellen Meiksins Wood* and David Harvey* investigate informal "covert" imperialism.*

- Post-Marxists* (thinkers who reject certain principles that are key to Marxist theory), such as the American political theorist Michael Hardt* and the Italian philosopher Antonio Negri,* argue that the empire of the twenty-first century is not dominated by one power but is rather a "state of affairs" where capitalism* itself dominates everywhere.

Uses and Problems

Hobson's core idea—the relationship between militarism,* capitalism, and imperialism—was developed by his fellow theorists of imperial power during the early twentieth century.

The most famous Marxist theorist attracted by Hobson's indictment of capitalist imperialism was Vladimir Lenin,* the first communist* premier of the Soviet Union.* Echoing Hobson, Lenin wrote: "Imperialism is the monopoly stage of capitalism … in which the export of capital has acquired pronounced importance."[1] The chief difference between the two thinkers involved the cure for

> **❝** We should emphasize that we use 'Empire' here not as a metaphor ... but rather as a concept, which calls primarily for a theoretical approach. The concept of Empire is characterized fundamentally by a lack of boundaries: Empire's rule has no limits. First and foremost, then, the concept of Empire posits a regime that effectively encompasses the spatial totality, or really that rules over the entire 'civilized' world. No territorial boundaries limit its reign. **❞**
>
> Michael Hardt and Antonio Negri, *Empire*

imperialism: Hobson held that the crisis could be overcome through redistribution, while Lenin believed that the only way to get rid of imperialism was to get rid of capitalism altogether.

And while the Austrian economist and political thinker Joseph Schumpeter* agreed that economic and military forces figured in imperialism, he turned Hobson's thesis on its head. Whereas Hobson believed that economic considerations in turn bred militarism, Schumpeter theorized that imperialism was rooted in militarism, with economic justifications applied after the fact. "Created by wars that required it, the [state war machine] now created the wars it required" by manufacturing economic justifications.[2] Schumpeter and Hobson agreed, however, on the illiberal* ramifications of militarism (that is, the consequences that compromised individual liberty).

The German political thinker Hannah Arendt* took this idea further, reemphasizing the ethical argument in her seminal work *The Origins of Totalitarianism*, where she wrote that imperialism resulted from the spread of capitalist thinking (and specifically the pursuit of unlimited growth) in the public sphere; that "expansion as a permanent and supreme aim of politics is the central idea of Imperialism."[3] Crucially for Arendt, the ideology of permanent expansion violated ethical and moral limits on politics—which echoed Hobson's concerns that imperial policy abroad damaged liberal* politics at home.

Schools of Thought

Hobson's scientific approach in *Imperialism* has attracted Marxists throughout history. But while they agreed in general that capitalist excess intertwined with imperialism, they disagreed on the root causes and cures for that overall condition. The Marxists were deterministic, believing that capitalism was an inevitable stage of history, with imperialism the final stage of capitalism. Thus a violent overthrow of capitalism and a cure for imperialism were the same thing—a sharp contrast to Hobson's appeal for a friendlier, equal form of capitalism.

The Polish German Marxist thinker Rosa Luxemburg based her theory of imperialism on the idea that "the colonial (developing) countries required finance from the capitalist countries for development in order to create markets for those capitalist countries."[4] Capitalism, in other words, will always need to open new markets to maintain profitability, meaning that capitalist states will fight over non-capitalist countries—"but the more violently, ruthlessly, and thoroughly Imperialism brings about the decline of non-capitalist civilizations, the more rapidly it cuts the ground from under the feet of capitalist accumulation."[5] Imperialism, in other words, is not just about exporting capital, but also about making more societies capitalist.

Late twentieth-century Marxists, especially the British social geographer David Harvey and the Canadian historian Ellen Meiksins Wood, contest the role of the state in imperial policy. They argue that while modern imperialism is largely non-territorial and non-expansionary, it relies on state hegemony* (or dominance) and the constant threat of military action.[6] Power defines "asymmetries of exchange relations [between more and less developed nations] … forcing open markets throughout the world by institutional pressures exercised through … [financial institutions such as the International

Monetary Fund* and the World Bank]* backed by the power of the United States ... to deny access to its own vast market."[7]

In Current Scholarship

The two most famous post-Marxist critics of empire are Michael Hardt and Antonio Negri. For both of them, the "Empire" is a globalized system defined by capitalism, but without a national center. The capitalist system benefits and awards privileges to some nation states over others (for example, the United States as compared with the developing world), but has also emerged as a network of international organizations such as the International Monetary Fund and the World Bank, transnational corporations, and social connections between the powerful.

In Hobson's thinking, capital propelled the nation state to do its bidding; in Hardt and Negri's thinking, capital has *superseded* the nation state. "The concept of Empire," they write, "is characterized fundamentally by a lack of boundaries: Empire's rule has no limits."[8] First, they argue, this means that empire encompasses the entire world; second, empire is no longer imposed by any one state, but is instead a "state of affairs"; and finally, "Empire operates on all registers of the social order extending down to the depths of the social world."[9] In their paradigm or model, the power of globalized* (worldwide) capitalism is not controlled by some powerful individuals at the expense of others, but is so powerful in and of itself that it controls the entire world's population of both "exploiters" and "exploited" by defining who they are and how they relate to one another.

In essence, Hardt and Negri have moved away from a number of Hobson's core ideas, such as the one-way relationship where capitalists and statesmen oppressed imperial subjects, and emphasize instead the ever-increasing power of capitalism. In Hobson, capitalism defined state policy; in Hardt and Negri, the ascent of capitalism is complete, and it has come to define everything, everywhere.

NOTES

1   Vladimir Lenin, *Imperialism: The Highest Stage of Capitalism* (New York: International Publishers, 1939), 88–9.

2   Joseph Schumpeter, *Imperialism and Social Classes: Two Essays*, trans. Heinz Norden (New York: Meridian, 2007), 25.

3   Hannah Arendt, *The Origins of Totalitarianism* (New York: Harcourt, 1968), 125.

4   Philip Arestis and Malcolm Sawyer, *The Elgar Companion to Radical Political Economy* (Aldershot: Edward Elgar, 1994), 21.

5   Rosa Luxemburg, *The Accumulation of Capital*, accessed February 22, 2014, http://www.marxists.org/archive/luxemburg/1913/accumulation-capital/ch31.htm.

6   Ellen Meiksins Wood, *Empire of Capital* (London: Verso, 2005), 130.

7   David Harvey, *The New Imperialism* (Oxford: Oxford University Press, 2005), 32.

8   Michael Hardt and Antonio Negri, *Empire* (Cambridge, MA: Harvard University Press, 2000), xv.

9   Hardt and Negri, *Empire*, xv.

MODULE 11
IMPACT AND INFLUENCE TODAY

KEY POINTS

- Hobson is no longer an "active" participant in today's debates—he is more important for his insight into the way private interests can subvert the state.

- According to neorealist* theories explaining international relations (that is, the interactions of nations), all foreign aggression by states results from rational power calculation; the social theorists David Harvey* and Ellen Meiksins Wood* respond by suggesting that the Iraq War* was politically irrational but economically sensible.

- According to neorealist theories of international relations, no state would take the chance of pursuing economic gains through war, as it is simply too risky; the United States fights abroad to reshape the world in its own image and guarantee its security.

Position

John Hobson's 1902 book *Imperialism: A Study* is no longer an active part of the current economic or political debate. In general, Hobson's role is appreciated less for his theory in itself than for his having inaugurated criticism of imperialism* as an economic, rather than a political, phenomenon that is in the interests of a minority.

The American economist Gregory Nowell's* treatment of Hobson gives an example of why this is so: "Are we still talking about Hobson? Yes and no. Hobson's core issues are oligarchy* [government by a minority], oligopoly* [the hold on a market by a small number of producers], their impact on the political system, their impact on the potential for social control over investment, and redistribution of

> ❝ The building blocks of Hobson's *Imperialism* were then and are now relevant for understanding capitalism. ❞
>
> Gregory Nowell, "Hobson's *Imperialism*," *The Political Economy of Imperialism*

income. This," Nowell writes, "is the true Hobson, who appeals to the modern reader, not the narrowly construed explicator of colonialism."[*1]

So while important for the study of history, and the history of ideas, Hobson's analysis of British imperialism is incidental to the perspectives of politics and economics—and this limits his analysis of capitalist* power.[2] Modern Marxists* such as David Harvey and Ellen Meiksins Wood reject Hobson's "conspiracy theory" in favor of a more general presumption that the interests of American enterprise and government are roughly aligned.[3] Both Harvey and Meiksins Wood take their inspiration from Hobson by analyzing the connection of military activity and capitalist expansion: "Boundless domination of a global economy," writes Meiksins Wood, "and of the multiple states that administer it, requires military action without end, in purpose or time."[4] In that spirit, both writers agree that imperialism is connected to the requirement of "global hegemony"* (that is, a dominant force), initiated either by a capitalist power (Harvey), or by a group of states in support of capitalism generally (Meiksins Wood).

Interaction

In his book *Theory of International Politics* (1979), the American political theorist Kenneth Waltz* offered a very critical analysis of Hobson's argument as he made the case for the neorealist school of thought.

Neorealism asserts that state action can always be understood in terms of relative power; that is, states try to maximize their power relative to other states, and powerful states pursue regional hegemony (dominance) as an end in itself.[5] These theorists would see post-Cold War* American dominance of global politics as an example of this.

In other words, neorealist thought, as set out by Kenneth Waltz and updated by the political theorist John Mearsheimer* in his book *The Tragedy of Great Power Politics* (2001), is a persuasive challenge to Hobson's analysis.

More recent theorists of imperial power, however, have responded to the neorealist idea that foreign conflict is driven by state security interests. David Harvey, for example, would counter that the neorealist position is mistaken to dismiss the invasion of Iraq as irrational, arguing that it was rational from a narrow, economic point of view.

"When Joseph Chamberlain* led Britain into the Boer War* ... at the beginning of the twentieth century," Harvey writes, "it was clear that gold and diamond reserves were the prime motivation." In turn, this would allow over-accumulated capital in Britain to be invested abroad.[6] Likewise, "the drive of the administration [of President George W. Bush*] to intervene militarily in the Middle East," he argues, "has to do with procuring firmer control over Middle Eastern oil resources ... [and] the general lowering of oil prices can be seen as one tactic in seeking to confront the chronic problems of over-accumulation that have arisen over the past three decades."[7]

Harvey argues that the Iraq War, like Hobson argued for the Boer War, was rational from the point of view of finance capitalism,* but irrational from the point of view of both public and strategic interests.[8]

Meiksins Wood contends that America's "economic empire would be sustained by political and military hegemony over a complex state system," concerned especially with opening a "third world that had to be made available to Western capital."[9] She also outlines her differences with Harvey's view of capitalist imperialism, saying "he argues that ever-expanding capital accumulation must be accompanied by an ever-expanding political power and command over territory, and that this is the logic of capitalist imperialism. I argue almost the reverse: the specificity of capitalist imperialism lies in the unique capacity of capital to impose its hegemony *without* expanding its territorial political power … Capitalism alone has created an autonomously *economic* form of domination."[10]

The Continuing Debate
Neorealism has challenged Hobson and the contemporary Marxists since its inception; in fact, Kenneth Waltz used *Imperialism* as an example of an incorrect theory. Waltz argued that many different kinds of states, including non-capitalist ones, have pursued imperial policies. "The acceptance of [Hobson's] theory," he states, was based on "the attractiveness of its economic reasoning and on the blatant truth that the advanced capitalist states of the day were, indeed, among history's most impressive builders of empire … Then why not identify capitalism with Imperialism?"[11] Waltz answers his own question this way: "All kinds of states," including the non-capitalist Soviet Union,* "have pursued Imperialist policies."[12] And therefore, the economic explanation should not trump reasons of grand strategy.

Mearsheimer agrees, to a point, that America is pursuing an imperialist foreign policy, and that this threatens domestic freedoms by encouraging militarism* and a "security culture."[13] Mearsheimer and Hobson also agree on the domestic point.[14] They disagree, however, on the reasons behind this imperial project, with Mearsheimer writing that "the root cause of America's troubles is that it adopted a flawed grand strategy after the Cold War … pursuing global dominance, or what might alternatively be called global hegemony."*[15]

But if economic objectives are not behind this plan, then what is? For Mearsheimer, the answer is evident: "Making sure that the United States remains the most powerful state in the international system; and spreading democracy across the globe, in effect, making the world in America's image."[16] In essence, modern neorealism believes that America pursues power with security in mind first and foremost, and with economic motivations irrelevant. So while critics of modern imperialism (such as Harvey and Meiksins Wood) see the 2003 invasion of Iraq as a rational pursuit of capitalist interests, Waltz and Mearsheimer see it only as a massive mistake.

NOTES

1   Gregory Nowell, "Hobson's *Imperialism*: Its Historical Validity and Contemporary Relevance," in *The Political Economy of Imperialism: Critical Appraisals* (Lanham, MD: Rowman and Littlefield, 1999), 102.

2   Nowell, "Hobson's *Imperialism*," 104.

3   David Harvey, *The New Imperialism* (Oxford: Oxford University Press, 2005), 18.

4   Ellen Meiksins Wood, *Empire of Capital* (London: Verso, 2005), 144.

5   John Mearsheimer, *The Tragedy of Great Power Politics* (New York: W. W. Norton, 2001), 169.

6   Harvey, *New Imperialism*, 180.

7   Harvey, *New Imperialism*, 180.

8   John Hobson, *Imperialism: A Study* (Nottingham: Spokesman, 2011), 85.

9   Meiksins Wood, *Empire of Capital*, 130.

10 Ellen Meiksins Wood, "Logics of Power: A Conversation with David Harvey," *Historical Materialism* 14, no. 4 (2006): 13.

11 Kenneth Waltz, *Theory of International Politics* (Reading, MA: Addison Wesley, 1979), 25.

12 Waltz, *Theory*, 36.

13 John Mearsheimer, "Imperial by Design," *The National Interest* 111 (2011): 17.

14 Hobson, *Imperialism*, 142.

15 Mearsheimer, "Imperial by Design," 18.

16 Mearsheimer, "Imperial by Design," 19.

MODULE 12
WHERE NEXT?

KEY POINTS

- Hobson's work will remain relevant as long as states pursue aggressive foreign policies that can be linked to economic gains.

- *Imperialism* will continue to be part of a long-standing tradition that accuses the capitalist* system of being "rigged" in favor of one class or another—the French economist Thomas Piketty's* book *Capital in the Twenty-First Century* can be seen as continuing this project.

- *Imperialism* is seminal not for its core argument, but for uncovering the network of relationships—even now poorly understood—that drive the engine of capitalist expansion.

Potential

The Canadian scholar Michael Ignatieff* has insisted that America's "war on terror"* is a rhetorical cover for an imperial project: he considers American foreign policy imperial even though it does not overtly annex territory abroad. "What else can you call America's legions of soldiers, spooks, and Special Forces straddling the globe" than an imperial force?[1] You could call it a ruse of sorts. This post-Hobson perspective sees the "war on terror" as a means to justify foreign intervention rather than as a true representation of America's security interests.

Additionally, Hobson's concept of imperialism* requires that the imperial project be rational for private economic interests—at the expense of the public interest. In his *Farewell Address,* US President Dwight D. Eisenhower* revealed this relationship between militarism, imperial expansion, and the price to the public. In fact, he memorably

> **"** This conjunction of an immense military establishment and a large arms industry is new in the American experience. The total influence—economic, political, even spiritual—is felt in every city, every State house, every office of the Federal government. **"**
>
> Dwight D. Eisenhower, *Farewell Address*

coined the phrase "military-industrial complex,"* warning: "In councils of government we must guard against the influence of the acquisition of unwarranted influence, sought or unsought, by the military-industrial complex."[2]

To allow this confluence of interests to control policy, according to Eisenhower, would decrease domestic liberty and increase militarism* abroad. And continuing anxiety over the complex is brought into the present day with an article published in the *Independent* newspaper in 2014, "Ike Was Right All Along," in which the British journalist Rupert Cornwell* writes: "The true tragedy is not quite the one that Eisenhower imagined. The US by itself accounts for roughly half of military spending worldwide. How much better if some of that money would be used to improve the country's education and infrastructure, or provide health care for all, or increase foreign aid, rather than protecting America from threats that geography alone renders illusory?"[3]

Hobson's assertion that militarism abroad would ultimately erode domestic liberty has made it into popular discourse. The American law scholar Jeffrey Rosen's* criticism of the USA PATRIOT Act* is an example. The acronym, which clearly invoked American patriotism,* stood for *Providing Appropriate Tools Required to Intercept and Obstruct Terrorism*—but it also cloaked the actions and dangers behind the law: "From the beginning, Democratic and Republican critics of the Patriot Act warned that its extraordinary surveillance powers would be used to investigate political dissent and low-level offences rather than terrorism. ... A 2007 report by the Inspector General of the Justice Department found 'widespread and serious abuse' of authority by the FBI [Federal Bureau of Investigation]* under the Patriot Act—even though these actions involved no clear connection to terrorism."[4]

Future Directions

One of the most exciting, ongoing aspects of the project Hobson initiated concerns economics.

The book by the French economist Thomas Piketty, *Capital in the Twenty-First Century* (2014), takes the premise that "there is no fundamental reason why we should believe that growth is automatically balanced," and that capitalist development leads to more inequality, rather than less.[5] Piketty's first major conclusion is that the distribution of wealth is not the result of "economic determinism"—there are no laws internal to the capitalist economic system that offer any guarantees about the distribution of wealth.[6]

Most importantly—in terms of pushing Hobson's idea to its natural conclusion—Piketty argues that "the history of the distribution of wealth has always been deeply political."[7] And so Piketty and Hobson's theories hold common ground in terms of how disproportionate political weight can be given to the interests of the wealthy. In Hobson's case, that is how the wealthy induce politicians to pursue imperial policies that secure their capital investments abroad; in Piketty's case, that is how political decisions on the distribution of wealth favor the interests of the wealthy.

Piketty's book makes another key assertion: those at the very top of major companies can, and often do, collude to act in their own interests, contrary to those of the public—and this is much akin to Hobson's conspiracy theory. But there are two important differences.

First, Piketty believes the collusion exists within the business world, rather than between business and government (as Hobson does). And second, Piketty's reasoning for this is clear, and not prone to slippage (as Hobson's is). But the two men argue that the nature of the collusion is actually very simple: "Top managers by and large have the power to set their own remuneration." They agree how much they are paid, in other words—and they happen to set that number very high indeed.[8]

In fact, a 2014 report by the American trade union* organization the American Federation of Labor and Congress of Industrial Organizations listed the pay of American chief executives at *331 times* that of the companies' employees—up from nearly 50 times in 1983.[9]

Summary

John Hobson's 1902 book *Imperialism: A Study* deserves special attention because it remains one of the most powerful and strident criticisms of imperial policy to come out of the tradition of British political radicalism.*

The work partly inspired Vladimir Lenin* to write his book *Capitalism is the Highest Stage of Imperialism*, and has served as a key inspiration for Marxist* thought from the twentieth century through to today. Even one of the book's harshest twentieth-century critics, the historian D. K. Fieldhouse,* credits *Imperialism* with a number of major achievements: Hobson demonstrated that imperialism was an irrational public policy, and encouraged "British, and subsequently world, opinion to accept his special definition of the word Imperialism."[10]

Hobson's "special" definition of imperialism involves more than just a military adventure beyond a nation's borders: it represents a capitalist project to open markets, exploit resources, and export capital. All of this, Hobson believed, amounts to a cynical enterprise that plays on public spiritedness to secure major gains for private investors—all at the expense of the public good both in the home country and in the colony.

While Hobson's analysis was largely discarded as conspiracy theory because it cast financiers* as larger-than-life power brokers over the state, it still boasts enough power to have taken on the status of a basic, foundational viewpoint. If anything, it is capitalism itself that has become larger than life—and thus for today's readers and thinkers, *Imperialism* holds value.

NOTES

1   Michael Ignatieff, "Nation Building Lite," *New York Times*, July 28, 2002, accessed February 22, 2014, http://www.nytimes.com/2002/07/28/magazine/nation-building-lite.html.

2   Dwight D. Eisenhower, *Farewell Address*, accessed February 17, 2014, http://www.americanrhetoric.com/speeches/dwightdeisenhowerfarewell.html.

3   Rupert Cornwell, "Ike Was Right All Along: The Danger of the Military Industrial Complex," January 17, 2011, accessed February 22, 2014, http://www.independent.co.uk/news/world/americas/ike-was-right-all-along-the-danger-of-the-militaryindustrial-complex-2186133.html.

4   Jeffrey Rosen, "Too Much Power?," *International New York Times*, September 7, 2007, accessed February 22, 2014, http://www.nytimes.com/roomfordebate/2011/09/07/do-we-still-need-the-patriot-act/the-patriot-act-gives-too-much-power-to-law-enforcement.

5   Thomas Piketty, Anthony Atkinson, and Emmanuel Saez, *Capital in the Twenty-First Century* (Cambridge, MA: Belknap Press, 2014), 15.

6   Piketty et al., *Capital*, 20.

7   Piketty et al., *Capital*, 20.

8   Piketty et al., *Capital*, 24.

9   "PayWatch 2014," AFL-CIO report, accessed July 9, 2015, http://edit.aflcio.org/Corporate-Watch/Paywatch-2014.

10 D. K. Fieldhouse, "Imperialism: A Historiographical Revision," *Economic History Review* 14, no. 2 (1961): 187.

GLOSSARY

GLOSSARY OF TERMS

Anti-Semitism: discrimination or hatred directed toward Jewish people.

Boer War (1899–1902): a conflict between the British Empire and the Boer Republics (lands in present-day South Africa then claimed and governed by the descendants of Dutch settlers—the Boers). The end of the war saw the Empire annex the Boer territories at considerable military and civilian cost to both sides.

Capitalism: an economic system in which the means of production (generally resources and factories) are owned as private property, with the goal of selling products to make profit in a market economy.

Classical liberalism: the political belief that the liberty of the individual ought to be maximized by limitation of state power; it advocates private property and minimal intervention.

Cold War (1947–91): a period of tension between the United States and the Soviet Union and aligned nations. While the two blocs never engaged in direct military conflict, they engaged in covert and proxy wars (sponsored opposing sides in military conflicts), and espionage against one another.

Colonialism: as Hobson understands it, colonialism occurs when a developed nation reproduces itself on otherwise unused land, extending full rights of citizenship to all those who move there. Hobson sees this as the opposite of imperialism.

Communism: a political ideology that relies on the state ownership of the means of production, collectivization of labor, and abolition of social class. It was the ideology of the Soviet Union (1917–89), and contrasted with free market capitalism during the Cold War.

Concentration camp: a camp where non-military, perceived enemies of the state are detained in poor conditions and often without trial.

Eurocentrism: the idea that European cultural history provides some kind of "standard" against which all others are judged.

Fabian Society: an English socialist organization founded in 1884, seeking to influence the parliamentary process through long-term pressure.

Federal Bureau of Investigation (FBI): an American governmental institution serving to investigate acts of espionage, terrorism, and major crime.

Finance capitalism: the aspect of a capitalist economy specifically concerned with finance (private investment made with the aim of private profit).

Financier: a person whose primary profession is investing in, owning, and lending large sums of money to business ventures.

Globalization: a number of processes of international integration (both planned and organic) that arise from a global interchange of ideas, culture, and material goods.

Hegemony: dominance in all forms over all others, especially by a state or military entity.

Illiberal: contrary to liberal political tenets: either unconcerned with promoting individual liberty or concerned with actively limiting individual liberty.

Imperialism: for Hobson, this is the forcible subjugation of one nationality in one territory by another for economic ends.

Institutional economics: the study of the role of previously existing institutions and ideas in shaping economic behavior.

International Monetary Fund (IMF): an international institution founded on the principle of promoting cooperation and good financial governance.

Iraq War (2003–11): an armed conflict initially fought between Iraq and the United States and its allies; once the initial military aims of the United States and its allies had been achieved, a protracted insurgency began. The justification for war was that Saddam Hussein, the leader of Iraq, was secretly building weapons of mass destruction. No such weapons were found.

Jingoism: aggressive patriotism.

Leninist imperialism: an understanding of imperialism expounded by the Russian revolutionary leader Vladimir Lenin that bears many similarities to that of Hobson. Lenin believed middle-class financiers exported capital to the developing world in order to exploit the poor. He differed from Hobson in concluding that this exploitation was to forestall revolution by the lower classes in the home country, and that revolution was the only solution to both capitalism and imperialism.

Liberal Party (1859–1988): a political party of the United Kingdom. It favored welfare and advancing trade. In 1988, it merged with the Social Democratic party to create the still-active Liberal Democratic Party.

Liberalism: an approach to politics that favors individual liberty and the promotion of welfare.

Marxism: a broad school of social analysis that is characterized by materialism, class conflict, and determinism, founded on the work of the German political philosopher Karl Marx.

Mercantilism: the dominant economic policy of Western Europe until the nineteenth century. It aimed for a positive balance of trade (meaning that trade should be primarily internal), and therefore was a key driver of colonial expansion.

Militarism: the belief that the military is the most important element of a state, and that the use of force is an appropriate (and often necessary) element of foreign policy.

Military-industrial complex: the network of relationships between American lawmakers, military general staff, and the private arms industry.

Nationalism: extreme patriotism, often paired with disdain for other nations.

Neorealism: a school of international relations theory which assumes that structural constraints—anarchy and the distribution of world power—will determine actor behavior rather than human agency.

New liberals: followers of liberal thought who favored government intervention to ensure economic social justice.

Oligarchy: a state of affairs in which a small number of individuals share power over others.

Oligopoly: a state of affairs in which a small number of producers share a market.

PATRIOT Act (2001): a piece of American legislation that allows law enforcement agencies unprecedented powers of surveillance of American citizens. Also known as the USA PATRIOT Act.

Patriotism: having love and reverence for one's own country.

Political economy: a branch of the academic discipline of economics. "Political economy" usually refers to the study of the ways that political systems and institutions affect the running of national economies.

Post-Marxism: a school of thought that builds on standard Marxist thought by rejecting a number of its key assumptions. For example, post-Marxists do not believe that capitalists use the state as a tool, as did Marx; for them, the notion of a "state" is inherently "capitalist."

Progressive taxation: a system where the tax rate increases as the taxable amount increases; the resulting average tax rate is less than the highest marginal tax rate.

Prototype: the "first run" of some product or service (usually done as a "proof of concept").

Radicalism (eighteenth to nineteenth century): a left-wing British political movement rooted in demands for reform of the electoral system to widen the franchise. It eventually encompassed multiple intellectual movements to increase political liberalism.

Say's Law: named for the French economist Jean-Baptiste Say (1767–1832), Say's Law argues that production is the source of demand. In other words, when an individual produces, he will be paid, and then purchase the production of others, who will in turn purchase his, and so on.

Scramble for Africa (1881–1914): a period of energetic expansion by European powers into African territories to claim direct rule of colonies and exploit the continent's resources.

Social Darwinism: the use of scientific language and the use of (supposedly) scientific techniques to support racist beliefs. It was notably practiced in Germany by the Nazi Party in the 1930s and 1940s as part of a racist/anti-Semitic political platform. The term has now taken on a pejorative meaning.

Social liberalism: the political belief that liberty (liberalism) ought to be managed by state organisms (socialism). Social liberals believe in a market economy as well as a redistributive program.

Socialism: the political belief that the factors of production of goods should be owned "socially" by the people, rather than by individual capitalists.

Soviet Union: a federation of communist states that existed between 1922 and 1991, centered primarily on Russia and its neighbors in

Eastern Europe and the northern half of Asia. It was the communist pole of the Cold War, with the United States as its main "rival."

Trade unionism: the organization of laborers in a common profession who come together to bargain with purchasers of their labor, and also to influence policy.

Underconsumption theory: the theory that economies stagnate due to inadequate demand relative to supply. It was largely replaced in the 1930s by Keynesian theories—that is, theories derived from the ideas of the economist John Maynard Keynes—of aggregate demand.

"War on terror": a term commonly applied to American-led actions throughout the Middle East against non-state "terrorist" actors, including al Qaeda and ISIS. The drone campaign in Pakistan, the occupation of Afghanistan, and other covert and overt operations are rolled into this effort.

World Bank: an international financial institution established to manage economic aid and make loans to members, allowing them to overcome financial crises.

World War I: also called the Great War, World War I was fought between 1914 and 1918. During the war, the Allied forces (led by France, Italy, Russia, the United Kingdom and the United States) and the Central powers (led by Austria-Hungary, Bulgaria, Germany, and the Ottoman Empire) fought, leaving 16 million people dead.

PEOPLE MENTIONED IN THE TEXT

Norman Angell (1872–1967) was an English lecturer and author, and a prominent member of the idealist school of international relations.

Hannah Arendt (1906–75) was a German political thinker. Her work deals with the nature of power and control.

Michael Barratt Brown (1918–2015) was a British political economist and Marxist scholar. He was particularly concerned with foreign policy.

Jeremy Bentham (1748–1832) was a British philosopher and liberal social reformer. He is considered the founding figure of the philosophy of utilitarianism (according to which, roughly, an action can be judged "good" if it serves to make people happy).

George W. Bush (b. 1946) is an American politician. He was the 43rd president of the United States, from 2001 to 2009. The attacks of September 11, 2001, the invasion of Iraq in 2003, and the ongoing occupation of Afghanistan occurred under his presidency.

P. J. Cain (b. 1941) is a British professor of history at Sheffield University. He specializes in the history of English liberal thought.

Joseph Chamberlain (1836–1914) was a British politician who served as secretary of state for the colonies, presiding over the Second Boer War.

Richard Cobden (1804–65) was a British businessman and Liberal statesman, and an advocate of a liberal conception of international politics.

Jeremy Corbyn (b. 1949) is a British member of parliament and leader of the Labour Party from September 2015.

Rupert Cornwell is a British journalist, notable as the chief US correspondent of London's *Independent*.

Dwight D. Eisenhower (1890–1969) was an American politician and general, and president of the United States (1953–61).

David Kenneth (D. K.) Fieldhouse (b. 1925) is a historian of the British Empire at Jesus College, Cambridge.

Thomas Hill Green (1836–82) was an English liberal philosopher. He is well known for the distinction he drew between negative liberty (the freedom of no restriction) and positive liberty (the freedom of being enabled).

Michael Hardt (b. 1960) is an American literary theorist and political philosopher.

David Harvey (b. 1935) is a British professor of geography specializing in social theory at the City University of New York. He is widely credited as one of the foremost Marxist critics of global capitalism.

Michael Ignatieff (b. 1947) is a Canadian academic specializing in international development, and is a former Liberal politician.

Baron John Maynard Keynes (1883–1946) was a British economist. He is widely referred to as the founder of modern macroeconomics for showing that perfectly free markets do not provide full employment.

Vladimir Lenin (1870–1924) was a Russian communist revolutionary politician. He was the first premier of the Soviet Union.

John Locke (1632–1704) was an English philosopher famous as one of the founders of classical liberalism, in which the freedom of the individual is emphasized and the power of the government is limited. He was a major thinker in the social contract school. His work *The Second Treatise on Government* is still widely considered groundbreaking.

David Long is a Canadian professor of international relations at Carleton University.

John Lonsdale is a historian and fellow of Trinity College, Cambridge specializing in African studies.

Rosa Luxemburg (1871–1919) was a Polish German Marxist thinker and founder of the predecessor to the Communist Party of Germany.

Lars Magnusson (b. 1952) is an economic historian at the University of Uppsala in Sweden. He is a key figure in the revival of Hobson scholarship.

Karl Marx (1818–83) was a German political philosopher famous for writing, among other works, *Capital* and *The Communist Manifesto*. His main idea, that human society progresses from one stage to the next through class struggle, sits at the core of Marxism.

John Mearsheimer (b. 1947) is an American international relations professor and neorealist. He is the pioneer of "offensive realism," a contemporary reformulation of neorealism.

Nathaniel Mehr is a British journalist, author, and left-wing public intellectual.

Ellen Meiksins Wood (b. 1942) is an American Marxist historian and scholar, formerly of York University in Canada.

John Stuart Mill (1806–73) was an English liberal philosopher and political economist. He was a key early proponent of the right of the citizen to live free from state interference.

Albert Mummery (1855–95) was a British businessman and mountaineer.

Antonio Negri (b. 1933) is an Italian Marxist philosopher and political agitator. After living in exile in France, where he taught at the Sorbonne, he returned to Italy in 1997 to serve a 13-year prison sentence (commuted from 30 years) for alleged anti-state activity.

Gregory Nowell is an American professor of political economy specializing in Marxism and the international oil industry at the State University of New York.

Thomas Piketty (b. 1971) is a French economist and best-selling author (best known for *Capital in the Twenty-First Century*). His book argues that in the long run, income generated from capital outstrips that generated from individual worker wages.

Cecil Rhodes (1853–1902) was a British tycoon and politician in South Africa. He established the diamond company De Beers, which today accounts for 40 percent of the world's diamond trade.

Jeffrey Rosen (b. 1964) is an American legal academic at Yale Law School.

John Ruskin (1819–1900) was a British art critic, social thinker, and philanthropist. His famous book *Unto This Last* (1860) argued for a social element of economic thought.

Jean-Baptiste Say (1767–1832) was a French economist and businessman who developed Say's Law, according to which production is the source of demand. It is a principle of classical economics (a theoretical approach to economics opposed to government interference in the economy).

Joseph Schumpeter (1883–1950) was an Austrian economist and political thinker who wrote on many areas; some of his most famous work is on innovation and business. He believed economies were driven forward through invention and "creative destruction" (horses and buggies, for example, were replaced by trains).

Adam Smith (1723–90) was a Scottish political philosopher widely considered to be the founding father of economics as an academic discipline with his book *The Wealth of Nations* (1776).

Thorstein Veblen (1857–1929) was an American economist, sociologist, and founding thinker of institutional economics, a school of thought that suggested that capitalism was inefficient due to its inbuilt holdovers (institutions) from the past.

Kenneth Waltz (1924–2013) was an American international relations professor best known for reformulating realism in order to make it more scientific (often called neorealism).

WORKS CITED

WORKS CITED

Arendt, Hannah. *The Origins of Totalitarianism*. New York: Harcourt, 1968.

Arestis, Philip, and Malcolm Sawyer. *The Elgar Companion to Radical Political Economy*. Aldershot: Edward Elgar, 1994.

Auld, John. "The Liberal Pro-Boers." *Journal of British Studies* 14, no. 2 (1975): 78–101.

Barratt Brown, Michael. *After Imperialism*. London: Merlin, 1970.

The Economics of Imperialism. London: Penguin, 1974.

Cain, P. J. *Hobson and Imperialism: Radicalism, New Liberalism, and Finance: 1887–1938*. Oxford: Oxford University Press, 2002.

"Radicalism, Gladstone and the Liberal Critique of Disraelian 'Imperialism.'" In *Victorian Visions of Global Order: Empire and International Relations in Nineteenth-Century Political Thought*, edited by Duncan Bell, 215–38. Cambridge: Cambridge University Press, 2007.

Cornwell, Rupert. "Ike Was Right All Along: The Danger of the Military Industrial Complex," January 17, 2011. Accessed February 22, 2014. http://www. independent.co.uk/news/world/americas/ike-was-right-all-along-the-danger-of-the-militaryindustrial-complex-2186133.html.

Cunningham Wood, John D., and Wood, Robert D. *John A. Hobson: Critical Assessments of Leading Economists*. London: Routledge, 2003.

Edgell, Stephen, and Jules Townshend. "John Hobson, Thorstein Veblen, and the Phenomenon of Imperialism: Finance Capital, Patriotism, and War." *American Journal of Economics and Sociology* 51, no. 4 (1992): 401–20.

Eisenhower, Dwight D. *Farewell Address*. Accessed February 17, 2014. http:// www.americanrhetoric.com/speeches/dwightdeisenhowerfarewell.html.

Fieldhouse, D. K. "Imperialism: An Historiographical Revision." *Economic History Review* 14, no. 2 (1961): 187–209.

Freeden, Michael. *Reappraising J. A. Hobson*. London: Unwin Hyman, 1990.

Green, T. H. "Liberal Legislation and Freedom of Contract." In *The Political Theory of T. H. Green: Selected Writings*, edited by John R. Rodman, 43–73. New York: Meredith, 1964.

Hardt, Michael, and Antonio Negri. *Empire*. Cambridge, MA: Harvard University Press, 2000.

Harvey, David. *The New Imperialism*. Oxford: Oxford University Press, 2005.

Hobson, John. *Confessions of an Economic Heretic*. Hassocks: Harvester Press, 1976.*The Evolution of Modern Capitalism*. London: The Walter Scott Publishing Company, 1906.

Imperialism: A Study. Nottingham: Spokesman, 2011.

The War in South Africa: Its Causes and Effects. London: James Nisbet and Co. Ltd, 1900.

Ignatieff, Michael. "Nation Building Lite." *New York Times*, July 28, 2002. Accessed February 22, 2014. http://www.nytimes.com/2002/07/28/magazine/nation-building-lite.html.

Jahn, Beate. "Kant, Mill, and Illiberal Legacies in International Affairs." *International Organization* 59, no. 1 (2005): 177–207.

Keynes, John Maynard. "Review of *Gold, Prices, and Wages*." *Economic Journal* 23 (1913): 393.

Lenin, Vladimir. *Imperialism: The Highest Stage of Capitalism*. New York: International Publishers, 1939.

Locke, John. *Second Treatise of Government*. Edited by C. B. Macpherson. Indianapolis, IN: Hackett, 1980.

Long, David. "Paternalism and the Internationalization of Imperialism: J. A. Hobson on the International Government of the 'Lower Races.'" In *Imperialism and Internationalism in the Discipline of International Relations*, edited by David Long and Brian Schmidt, 71–93. Albany, NY: University of New York Press, 2005.

Lonsdale, John. "The European Scramble and Conquest in African History." In *The Cambridge History of Africa*. Vol. 6, *c. 1870–c. 1905*, edited by Roland Oliver and G. N. Sanderson, 680–766. Cambridge: Cambridge University Press, 1985.

Luxemburg, Rosa. *The Accumulation of Capital*. Accessed February 22, 2014. http://www.marxists.org/archive/luxemburg/1913/accumulation-capital/ch31.htm.

Magnusson, Lars. "Hobson and Imperialism: An Appraisal." In *J. A. Hobson after Fifty Years*, edited by John Pheby, 143–62. London: Macmillan, 1994.

Mearsheimer, John. "Imperial by Design." *The National Interest* 111 (2011): 16–34.

The Tragedy of Great Power Politics. New York: W. W. Norton, 2001.

Meiksins Wood, Ellen. *Empire of Capital*. London: Verso, 2005.

"Logics of Power: A Conversation with David Harvey." *Historical Materialism* 14, no. 4 (2006): 9–34.

Mill, John Stuart. *Principles of Political Economy with Some of Their Applications to Social Philosophy*. London: Longmans, 1865.

Mitchell, Harvey. "Hobson Revisited." *Journal of the History of Ideas* 26, no. 3 (1965): 397–416.

Morgan, Kenneth. "The Boer War and the Media." *Twentieth Century British History* 13, no. 1 (2002): 1–16.

Mummery, Albert, and John Hobson. *The Physiology of Industry; Being an Exposure of Certain Fallacies in Existing Theories of Economics*. London: John Murray, 1889.

Nowell, Gregory. "Hobson's *Imperialism*: Its Historical Validity and Contemporary Relevance." In *The Political Economy of Imperialism: Critical Appraisals*, edited by Ronald H. Chilcote, 85–109. Lanham, MD: Rowman and Littlefield, 1999.

Oliver, Roland, and Atmore, Anthony. *Africa since 1800*. Cambridge: Cambridge University Press, 2005.

Piketty, Thomas, Anthony Atkinson, and Emmanuel Saez. *Capital in the Twenty-First Century*. Cambridge, MA: Belknap Press, 2014.

Porter, Bernard. *Critics of Empire: British Radicals and the Imperial Challenge*. London: I. B. Tauris, 2007.

Robertson, J. M. *Patriotism and Empire*. London: Grant Richards, 1900.

Rosen, Jeffrey. "Too Much Power?" *International New York Times*, September 7, 2007. Accessed February 22, 2014. http://www.nytimes.com/roomfordebate/2011/09/07/do-we-still-need-the-patriot-act/the-patriot-act-gives-too-much-power-to-law-enforcement.

Särkkä, Timo. *Hobson's Imperialism: A Study in Late Victorian Political Thought*. Jyväskylä: University of Jyväskylä, 2009.

Schneider, Michael. *J. A. Hobson*. London: Macmillan, 1996.

Schumpeter, Joseph. *Imperialism and Social Classes: Two Essays*. Translated by Heinz Norden. New York: Meridian, 2007.

Smith, Adam. *An Inquiry into the Nature and Causes of the Wealth of Nations*. London: Digireads, 2009.

Sullivan, Eileen. "Liberalism and Imperialism: J. S. Mill's Defence of the British Empire." *Journal of the History of Ideas* 44, no. 4 (1983): 599–617.

Veblen, Thorstein. *Absentee Ownership and Business Enterprise in Recent Times*. New York: Kelley, 1964.

Waltz, Kenneth. *Theory of International Politics*. Reading, MA: Addison Wesley, 1979.

THE MACAT LIBRARY
BY DISCIPLINE

The Macat Library By Discipline

AFRICANA STUDIES

Chinua Achebe's *An Image of Africa: Racism in Conrad's Heart of Darkness*
W. E. B. Du Bois's *The Souls of Black Folk*
Zora Neale Huston's *Characteristics of Negro Expression*
Martin Luther King Jr's *Why We Can't Wait*
Toni Morrison's *Playing in the Dark: Whiteness in the American Literary Imagination*

ANTHROPOLOGY

Arjun Appadurai's *Modernity at Large: Cultural Dimensions of Globalisation*
Philippe Ariès's *Centuries of Childhood*
Franz Boas's *Race, Language and Culture*
Kim Chan & Renée Mauborgne's *Blue Ocean Strategy*
Jared Diamond's *Guns, Germs & Steel: the Fate of Human Societies*
Jared Diamond's *Collapse: How Societies Choose to Fail or Survive*
E. E. Evans-Pritchard's *Witchcraft, Oracles and Magic Among the Azande*
James Ferguson's *The Anti-Politics Machine*
Clifford Geertz's *The Interpretation of Cultures*
David Graeber's *Debt: the First 5000 Years*
Karen Ho's *Liquidated: An Ethnography of Wall Street*
Geert Hofstede's *Culture's Consequences: Comparing Values, Behaviors, Institutes and Organizations across Nations*
Claude Lévi-Strauss's *Structural Anthropology*
Jay Macleod's *Ain't No Makin' It: Aspirations and Attainment in a Low-Income Neighborhood*
Saba Mahmood's *The Politics of Piety: The Islamic Revival and the Feminist Subject*
Marcel Mauss's *The Gift*

BUSINESS

Jean Lave & Etienne Wenger's *Situated Learning*
Theodore Levitt's *Marketing Myopia*
Burton G. Malkiel's *A Random Walk Down Wall Street*
Douglas McGregor's *The Human Side of Enterprise*
Michael Porter's *Competitive Strategy: Creating and Sustaining Superior Performance*
John Kotter's *Leading Change*
C. K. Prahalad & Gary Hamel's *The Core Competence of the Corporation*

CRIMINOLOGY

Michelle Alexander's *The New Jim Crow: Mass Incarceration in the Age of Colorblindness*
Michael R. Gottfredson & Travis Hirschi's *A General Theory of Crime*
Richard Herrnstein & Charles A. Murray's *The Bell Curve: Intelligence and Class Structure in American Life*
Elizabeth Loftus's *Eyewitness Testimony*
Jay Macleod's *Ain't No Makin' It: Aspirations and Attainment in a Low-Income Neighborhood*
Philip Zimbardo's *The Lucifer Effect*

ECONOMICS

Janet Abu-Lughod's *Before European Hegemony*
Ha-Joon Chang's *Kicking Away the Ladder*
David Brion Davis's *The Problem of Slavery in the Age of Revolution*
Milton Friedman's *The Role of Monetary Policy*
Milton Friedman's *Capitalism and Freedom*
David Graeber's *Debt: the First 5000 Years*
Friedrich Hayek's *The Road to Serfdom*
Karen Ho's *Liquidated: An Ethnography of Wall Street*

John Maynard Keynes's *The General Theory of Employment, Interest and Money*
Charles P. Kindleberger's *Manias, Panics and Crashes*
Robert Lucas's *Why Doesn't Capital Flow from Rich to Poor Countries?*
Burton G. Malkiel's *A Random Walk Down Wall Street*
Thomas Robert Malthus's *An Essay on the Principle of Population*
Karl Marx's *Capital*
Thomas Piketty's *Capital in the Twenty-First Century*
Amartya Sen's *Development as Freedom*
Adam Smith's *The Wealth of Nations*
Nassim Nicholas Taleb's *The Black Swan: The Impact of the Highly Improbable*
Amos Tversky's & Daniel Kahneman's *Judgment under Uncertainty: Heuristics and Biases*
Mahbub Ul Haq's *Reflections on Human Development*
Max Weber's *The Protestant Ethic and the Spirit of Capitalism*

FEMINISM AND GENDER STUDIES

Judith Butler's *Gender Trouble*
Simone De Beauvoir's *The Second Sex*
Michel Foucault's *History of Sexuality*
Betty Friedan's *The Feminine Mystique*
Saba Mahmood's *The Politics of Piety: The Islamic Revival and the Feminist Subject*
Joan Wallach Scott's *Gender and the Politics of History*
Mary Wollstonecraft's *A Vindication of the Rights of Women*
Virginia Woolf's *A Room of One's Own*

GEOGRAPHY

The Brundtland Report's *Our Common Future*
Rachel Carson's *Silent Spring*
Charles Darwin's *On the Origin of Species*
James Ferguson's *The Anti-Politics Machine*
Jane Jacobs's *The Death and Life of Great American Cities*
James Lovelock's *Gaia: A New Look at Life on Earth*
Amartya Sen's *Development as Freedom*
Mathis Wackernagel & William Rees's *Our Ecological Footprint*

HISTORY

Janet Abu-Lughod's *Before European Hegemony*
Benedict Anderson's *Imagined Communities*
Bernard Bailyn's *The Ideological Origins of the American Revolution*
Hanna Batatu's *The Old Social Classes And The Revolutionary Movements Of Iraq*
Christopher Browning's *Ordinary Men: Reserve Police Batallion 101 and the Final Solution in Poland*
Edmund Burke's *Reflections on the Revolution in France*
William Cronon's *Nature's Metropolis: Chicago And The Great West*
Alfred W. Crosby's *The Columbian Exchange*
Hamid Dabashi's *Iran: A People Interrupted*
David Brion Davis's *The Problem of Slavery in the Age of Revolution*
Nathalie Zemon Davis's *The Return of Martin Guerre*
Jared Diamond's *Guns, Germs & Steel: the Fate of Human Societies*
Frank Dikotter's *Mao's Great Famine*
John W Dower's *War Without Mercy: Race And Power In The Pacific War*
W. E. B. Du Bois's *The Souls of Black Folk*
Richard J. Evans's *In Defence of History*
Lucien Febvre's *The Problem of Unbelief in the 16th Century*
Sheila Fitzpatrick's *Everyday Stalinism*

Eric Foner's *Reconstruction: America's Unfinished Revolution, 1863-1877*
Michel Foucault's *Discipline and Punish*
Michel Foucault's *History of Sexuality*
Francis Fukuyama's *The End of History and the Last Man*
John Lewis Gaddis's *We Now Know: Rethinking Cold War History*
Ernest Gellner's *Nations and Nationalism*
Eugene Genovese's *Roll, Jordan, Roll: The World the Slaves Made*
Carlo Ginzburg's *The Night Battles*
Daniel Goldhagen's *Hitler's Willing Executioners*
Jack Goldstone's *Revolution and Rebellion in the Early Modern World*
Antonio Gramsci's *The Prison Notebooks*
Alexander Hamilton, John Jay & James Madison's *The Federalist Papers*
Christopher Hill's *The World Turned Upside Down*
Carole Hillenbrand's *The Crusades: Islamic Perspectives*
Thomas Hobbes's *Leviathan*
Eric Hobsbawm's *The Age Of Revolution*
John A. Hobson's *Imperialism: A Study*
Albert Hourani's *History of the Arab Peoples*
Samuel P. Huntington's *The Clash of Civilizations and the Remaking of World Order*
C. L. R. James's *The Black Jacobins*
Tony Judt's *Postwar: A History of Europe Since 1945*
Ernst Kantorowicz's *The King's Two Bodies: A Study in Medieval Political Theology*
Paul Kennedy's *The Rise and Fall of the Great Powers*
Ian Kershaw's *The "Hitler Myth": Image and Reality in the Third Reich*
John Maynard Keynes's *The General Theory of Employment, Interest and Money*
Charles P. Kindleberger's *Manias, Panics and Crashes*
Martin Luther King Jr's *Why We Can't Wait*
Henry Kissinger's *World Order: Reflections on the Character of Nations and the Course of History*
Thomas Kuhn's *The Structure of Scientific Revolutions*
Georges Lefebvre's *The Coming of the French Revolution*
John Locke's *Two Treatises of Government*
Niccolò Machiavelli's *The Prince*
Thomas Robert Malthus's *An Essay on the Principle of Population*
Mahmood Mamdani's *Citizen and Subject: Contemporary Africa And The Legacy Of Late Colonialism*
Karl Marx's *Capital*
Stanley Milgram's *Obedience to Authority*
John Stuart Mill's *On Liberty*
Thomas Paine's *Common Sense*
Thomas Paine's *Rights of Man*
Geoffrey Parker's *Global Crisis: War, Climate Change and Catastrophe in the Seventeenth Century*
Jonathan Riley-Smith's *The First Crusade and the Idea of Crusading*
Jean-Jacques Rousseau's *The Social Contract*
Joan Wallach Scott's *Gender and the Politics of History*
Theda Skocpol's *States and Social Revolutions*
Adam Smith's *The Wealth of Nations*
Timothy Snyder's *Bloodlands: Europe Between Hitler and Stalin*
Sun Tzu's *The Art of War*
Keith Thomas's *Religion and the Decline of Magic*
Thucydides's *The History of the Peloponnesian War*
Frederick Jackson Turner's *The Significance of the Frontier in American History*
Odd Arne Westad's *The Global Cold War: Third World Interventions And The Making Of Our Times*

LITERATURE

Chinua Achebe's *An Image of Africa: Racism in Conrad's Heart of Darkness*
Roland Barthes's *Mythologies*
Homi K. Bhabha's *The Location of Culture*
Judith Butler's *Gender Trouble*
Simone De Beauvoir's *The Second Sex*
Ferdinand De Saussure's *Course in General Linguistics*
T. S. Eliot's *The Sacred Wood: Essays on Poetry and Criticism*
Zora Neale Huston's *Characteristics of Negro Expression*
Toni Morrison's *Playing in the Dark: Whiteness in the American Literary Imagination*
Edward Said's *Orientalism*
Gayatri Chakravorty Spivak's *Can the Subaltern Speak?*
Mary Wollstonecraft's *A Vindication of the Rights of Women*
Virginia Woolf's *A Room of One's Own*

PHILOSOPHY

Elizabeth Anscombe's *Modern Moral Philosophy*
Hannah Arendt's *The Human Condition*
Aristotle's *Metaphysics*
Aristotle's *Nicomachean Ethics*
Edmund Gettier's *Is Justified True Belief Knowledge?*
Georg Wilhelm Friedrich Hegel's *Phenomenology of Spirit*
David Hume's *Dialogues Concerning Natural Religion*
David Hume's *The Enquiry for Human Understanding*
Immanuel Kant's *Religion within the Boundaries of Mere Reason*
Immanuel Kant's *Critique of Pure Reason*
Søren Kierkegaard's *The Sickness Unto Death*
Søren Kierkegaard's *Fear and Trembling*
C. S. Lewis's *The Abolition of Man*
Alasdair MacIntyre's *After Virtue*
Marcus Aurelius's *Meditations*
Friedrich Nietzsche's *On the Genealogy of Morality*
Friedrich Nietzsche's *Beyond Good and Evil*
Plato's *Republic*
Plato's *Symposium*
Jean-Jacques Rousseau's *The Social Contract*
Gilbert Ryle's *The Concept of Mind*
Baruch Spinoza's *Ethics*
Sun Tzu's *The Art of War*
Ludwig Wittgenstein's *Philosophical Investigations*

POLITICS

Benedict Anderson's *Imagined Communities*
Aristotle's *Politics*
Bernard Bailyn's *The Ideological Origins of the American Revolution*
Edmund Burke's *Reflections on the Revolution in France*
John C. Calhoun's *A Disquisition on Government*
Ha-Joon Chang's *Kicking Away the Ladder*
Hamid Dabashi's *Iran: A People Interrupted*
Hamid Dabashi's *Theology of Discontent: The Ideological Foundation of the Islamic Revolution in Iran*
Robert Dahl's *Democracy and its Critics*
Robert Dahl's *Who Governs?*
David Brion Davis's *The Problem of Slavery in the Age of Revolution*

Alexis De Tocqueville's *Democracy in America*
James Ferguson's *The Anti-Politics Machine*
Frank Dikotter's *Mao's Great Famine*
Sheila Fitzpatrick's *Everyday Stalinism*
Eric Foner's *Reconstruction: America's Unfinished Revolution, 1863-1877*
Milton Friedman's *Capitalism and Freedom*
Francis Fukuyama's *The End of History and the Last Man*
John Lewis Gaddis's *We Now Know: Rethinking Cold War History*
Ernest Gellner's *Nations and Nationalism*
David Graeber's *Debt: the First 5000 Years*
Antonio Gramsci's *The Prison Notebooks*
Alexander Hamilton, John Jay & James Madison's *The Federalist Papers*
Friedrich Hayek's *The Road to Serfdom*
Christopher Hill's *The World Turned Upside Down*
Thomas Hobbes's *Leviathan*
John A. Hobson's *Imperialism: A Study*
Samuel P. Huntington's *The Clash of Civilizations and the Remaking of World Order*
Tony Judt's *Postwar: A History of Europe Since 1945*
David C. Kang's *China Rising: Peace, Power and Order in East Asia*
Paul Kennedy's *The Rise and Fall of Great Powers*
Robert Keohane's *After Hegemony*
Martin Luther King Jr.'s *Why We Can't Wait*
Henry Kissinger's *World Order: Reflections on the Character of Nations and the Course of History*
John Locke's *Two Treatises of Government*
Niccolò Machiavelli's *The Prince*
Thomas Robert Malthus's *An Essay on the Principle of Population*
Mahmood Mamdani's *Citizen and Subject: Contemporary Africa And The Legacy Of Late Colonialism*
Karl Marx's *Capital*
John Stuart Mill's *On Liberty*
John Stuart Mill's *Utilitarianism*
Hans Morgenthau's *Politics Among Nations*
Thomas Paine's *Common Sense*
Thomas Paine's *Rights of Man*
Thomas Piketty's *Capital in the Twenty-First Century*
Robert D. Putman's *Bowling Alone*
John Rawls's *Theory of Justice*
Jean-Jacques Rousseau's *The Social Contract*
Theda Skocpol's *States and Social Revolutions*
Adam Smith's *The Wealth of Nations*
Sun Tzu's *The Art of War*
Henry David Thoreau's *Civil Disobedience*
Thucydides's *The History of the Peloponnesian War*
Kenneth Waltz's *Theory of International Politics*
Max Weber's *Politics as a Vocation*
Odd Arne Westad's *The Global Cold War: Third World Interventions And The Making Of Our Times*

POSTCOLONIAL STUDIES

Roland Barthes's *Mythologies*
Frantz Fanon's *Black Skin, White Masks*
Homi K. Bhabha's *The Location of Culture*
Gustavo Gutiérrez's *A Theology of Liberation*
Edward Said's *Orientalism*
Gayatri Chakravorty Spivak's *Can the Subaltern Speak?*

PSYCHOLOGY

Gordon Allport's *The Nature of Prejudice*
Alan Baddeley & Graham Hitch's *Aggression: A Social Learning Analysis*
Albert Bandura's *Aggression: A Social Learning Analysis*
Leon Festinger's *A Theory of Cognitive Dissonance*
Sigmund Freud's *The Interpretation of Dreams*
Betty Friedan's *The Feminine Mystique*
Michael R. Gottfredson & Travis Hirschi's *A General Theory of Crime*
Eric Hoffer's *The True Believer: Thoughts on the Nature of Mass Movements*
William James's *Principles of Psychology*
Elizabeth Loftus's *Eyewitness Testimony*
A. H. Maslow's *A Theory of Human Motivation*
Stanley Milgram's *Obedience to Authority*
Steven Pinker's *The Better Angels of Our Nature*
Oliver Sacks's *The Man Who Mistook His Wife For a Hat*
Richard Thaler & Cass Sunstein's *Nudge: Improving Decisions About Health, Wealth and Happiness*
Amos Tversky's *Judgment under Uncertainty: Heuristics and Biases*
Philip Zimbardo's *The Lucifer Effect*

SCIENCE

Rachel Carson's *Silent Spring*
William Cronon's *Nature's Metropolis: Chicago And The Great West*
Alfred W. Crosby's *The Columbian Exchange*
Charles Darwin's *On the Origin of Species*
Richard Dawkin's *The Selfish Gene*
Thomas Kuhn's *The Structure of Scientific Revolutions*
Geoffrey Parker's *Global Crisis: War, Climate Change and Catastrophe in the Seventeenth Century*
Mathis Wackernagel & William Rees's *Our Ecological Footprint*

SOCIOLOGY

Michelle Alexander's *The New Jim Crow: Mass Incarceration in the Age of Colorblindness*
Gordon Allport's *The Nature of Prejudice*
Albert Bandura's *Aggression: A Social Learning Analysis*
Hanna Batatu's *The Old Social Classes And The Revolutionary Movements Of Iraq*
Ha-Joon Chang's *Kicking Away the Ladder*
W. E. B. Du Bois's *The Souls of Black Folk*
Émile Durkheim's *On Suicide*
Frantz Fanon's *Black Skin, White Masks*
Frantz Fanon's *The Wretched of the Earth*
Eric Foner's *Reconstruction: America's Unfinished Revolution, 1863-1877*
Eugene Genovese's *Roll, Jordan, Roll: The World the Slaves Made*
Jack Goldstone's *Revolution and Rebellion in the Early Modern World*
Antonio Gramsci's *The Prison Notebooks*
Richard Herrnstein & Charles A Murray's *The Bell Curve: Intelligence and Class Structure in American Life*
Eric Hoffer's *The True Believer: Thoughts on the Nature of Mass Movements*
Jane Jacobs's *The Death and Life of Great American Cities*
Robert Lucas's *Why Doesn't Capital Flow from Rich to Poor Countries?*
Jay Macleod's *Ain't No Makin' It: Aspirations and Attainment in a Low Income Neighborhood*
Elaine May's *Homeward Bound: American Families in the Cold War Era*
Douglas McGregor's *The Human Side of Enterprise*
C. Wright Mills's *The Sociological Imagination*

Thomas Piketty's *Capital in the Twenty-First Century*
Robert D. Putman's *Bowling Alone*
David Riesman's *The Lonely Crowd: A Study of the Changing American Character*
Edward Said's *Orientalism*
Joan Wallach Scott's *Gender and the Politics of History*
Theda Skocpol's *States and Social Revolutions*
Max Weber's *The Protestant Ethic and the Spirit of Capitalism*

THEOLOGY

Augustine's *Confessions*
Benedict's *Rule of St Benedict*
Gustavo Gutiérrez's *A Theology of Liberation*
Carole Hillenbrand's *The Crusades: Islamic Perspectives*
David Hume's *Dialogues Concerning Natural Religion*
Immanuel Kant's *Religion within the Boundaries of Mere Reason*
Ernst Kantorowicz's *The King's Two Bodies: A Study in Medieval Political Theology*
Søren Kierkegaard's *The Sickness Unto Death*
C. S. Lewis's *The Abolition of Man*
Saba Mahmood's *The Politics of Piety: The Islamic Revival and the Feminist Subject*
Baruch Spinoza's *Ethics*
Keith Thomas's *Religion and the Decline of Magic*

COMING SOON

Chris Argyris's *The Individual and the Organisation*
Seyla Benhabib's *The Rights of Others*
Walter Benjamin's *The Work Of Art in the Age of Mechanical Reproduction*
John Berger's *Ways of Seeing*
Pierre Bourdieu's *Outline of a Theory of Practice*
Mary Douglas's *Purity and Danger*
Roland Dworkin's *Taking Rights Seriously*
James G. March's *Exploration and Exploitation in Organisational Learning*
Ikujiro Nonaka's *A Dynamic Theory of Organizational Knowledge Creation*
Griselda Pollock's *Vision and Difference*
Amartya Sen's *Inequality Re-Examined*
Susan Sontag's *On Photography*
Yasser Tabbaa's *The Transformation of Islamic Art*
Ludwig von Mises's *Theory of Money and Credit*